FREE
WHITE
AND
CHRISTIAN

FREE
WHITE
AND
CHRISTIAN

Donald G. Shockley

NASHVILLE **ABINGDON PRESS** NEW YORK

FREE, WHITE, AND CHRISTIAN

Copyright © 1975 by Abingdon Press

Library of Congress Cataloging in Publication Data

SHOCKLEY, DONALD G. 1937-
  Free, white, and Christian.
  Includes bibliographical references.
  1. Church and race problems—United States. 2. Protestant
churches—United States. 3. United States—Race question.
I. Title.
BR517.S42   261.8′34′51042   74-19276

ISBN 0-687-13502-8

Excerpts on page 82 from *Death of a Salesman* by Arthur
Miller. Copyright 1949 by Arthur Miller. Reprinted by permission of The Viking Press, Inc.

Excerpts on page 90 from *J.B.* by Archibald Macleish, published
by Houghton Mifflin Company, and used here with permission.

Excerpts on page 92 from the poem "Transcription of Organ
Music" in *Howl and Other Poems*. Copyright © 1956, 1959
by Allen Ginsberg. Reprinted by permission of City Lights
Books.

Parts of chapter 8 reprinted from *Christian Advocate*, January
7, 1971. Copyright © 1971 by The Methodist Publishing House.

Scripture quotations unless otherwise noted are from the Revised
Standard Version of the Bible, copyrighted 1946, 1952, and 1971
by the Division of Christian Education, National Council of
Churches, and are used by permission.

MANUFACTURED BY THE PARTHENON PRESS AT
NASHVILLE, TENNESSEE, UNITED STATES OF AMERICA

For Mary Jim

Contents

Acknowledgments

Whenever someone asks me how much time I devote to preparing a sermon, I usually answer with my current age. Certainly I could say of this book that it has been in preparation for more than thirty-six years, for I have self-consciously employed the recollection of people, places, and events as a primary resource for theological reflection. In the process of writing in this fashion the debt of gratitude one owes to more people than he can name becomes acutely apparent.

The specific occasion during which the idea for this book took shape was a sabbatical year spent at the San Francisco Theological Seminary. I am grateful to Birmingham-Southern College for the released time from my duties as chaplain and assistant professor of religion on that campus. Most importantly, I should acknowledge the awarding of a Danforth Campus Ministry Grant without which that year of study would have been impossible. Along with campus ministers all over America, I will always be indebted to the Danforth Foundation's Robert Rankin for his extraordinary contributions to our profession.

The Advanced Pastoral Studies program of the San Francisco Theological Seminary, directed by John S. Hadsell, has provided a unique means of relating sound academic inquiry to professional experience, and the interaction with students and teachers in that program has been of incalculable value to me in the preparation of this book. Professor Benjamin Reist has been particularly helpful in guiding the development of my interest in the relationship between theology and ethnic identity. As an adjunct professor to the APS program, Dr. Charles McCoy of the Pacific School of Religion read a portion of this manuscript at an early stage in its development and made comments which were most helpful.

In the pages which follow, I make reference to my first year in seminary as a kind of dark night of the soul through which I had to pass. Although I would like to absolve them of responsibility for what I have done with the things they taught me, three of my teachers at Emory University's School of Theology played crucial roles in my realization that intellectual curiosity and Christian faith need not be incompatible: Theodore Runyon in theology; Norman Perrin in New Testament studies; and William Mallard in church history. Without their contributions to my life at a critical juncture I doubt that I would be struggling today with the implications of Christian commitment for life in contemporary America.

I feel so indebted to so many at Birmingham-Southern College that I hesitate to name any of my colleagues and friends at the institution which I was privileged to serve for eight years as chaplain. But I must acknowledge the contributions of Imogene Newsom who not only typed portions of this manuscript at various stages of its development, but constantly encouraged me to keep on writing. During a very lean year in which I had no funds at all for secretarial assistance, Debbie G. DeBoer worked in the chaplain's office day after day on a volunteer basis. An extraordinary individual, she provided the calmness and confidence which helped to keep me within the company of the sane during some very difficult days at the college.

This manuscript in its final form was typed by my present secretary at the University of Redlands, Doris Howard, for whose daily labors I am most appreciative. I would like also to express my gratitude to Brent Waters, a student at this university, and to David Bond, a student at Johnston College, who read the manuscript and made helpful suggestions.

Without the understanding and enthusiastic support of my wife, Mary Jim, I could not have written this book. Her sympathetic listening and reading and her thoughtful conversation at every step of the way have been invaluable. Our children, Scott, James, and Allison, have undergirded my efforts with love and understanding, and each has sought to help me in his or her own way.

Having written much of this book from an autobiographical perspective, I am more conscious now than ever of the immeasurable debt I owe to my parents, Ira and Maggie B. Shockley. And there are many others whose names must be left unsaid here, but whose lives have touched my own in profoundly significant ways. Although much of what I have to say in the pages which follow may be unsettling to many people I love very much, I trust that they will see beneath it all an honest struggle to follow the One of whom they themselves have so often spoken.

Donald Shockley

I.
Religion and the Second American Revolution

Birmingham's My Home

The words in the dust on my old Volkswagen van would not have affected me so much under normal circumstances, but the circumstances at the time were anything but normal. With my wife, our three children, and two cats, I had left the city where I had lived all my life and driven the two thousand miles to California. We had come to stay, and we were a little anxious about how we would be received. Well, someone had cast an early vote in the finger-written words on the van: REDNECK GO HOME!

In retrospect, I am glad the inscription was there for several reasons, not least of all because the sentiment it expressed was by no means characteristic of the warm and friendly reception we received from our new colleagues and friends! But I thought at the time, given all that has happened in recent years, it was understandable that the sight of an Alabama license plate might cause someone a momentary flush of resentment and anger. After all, when I think of home, I think of a city which at its lowest point experienced the hate-inspired bombing of a church, resulting in death for four children and injury to others. Birmingham, Montgomery, Selma, Tuscaloosa: all at one time or another

infamous names in the early years of the civil rights movement, and all symbolized, I suppose, by that Alabama tag
with "Heart of Dixie" embossed along the bottom.

Beyond all those considerations, however, was the curious
sense of identity which had been building in me for several
years and was now brought into sharper focus. Whether we
are conscious of it or not, where we have come from is an
important part of the emotional freight we carry around
with us at all times. This is not to speak of geography as such,
but of the portable personal past we have each accumulated
and the past we have in common with others. James Baldwin
puts it this way:

> Even the most incorrigible maverick has to be born somewhere.
> He may leave the group that produced him—he may be forced
> to—but nothing will efface his origins, the marks of which he
> carries with him everywhere. I think it is important to know
> this and even find it a matter for rejoicing.[1]

After years of resentment and rebellion I was beginning to
come to terms with some basic facts of my biography in a
way which was helping me to "find it a matter for rejoicing."

When I was a boy, it was not possible to grow up in the
South without having instilled within your consciousness the
sense that you belonged to a special place and a special people. If it was good to be an American, it was especially good
to be a Southerner! In elementary school I was taught this
awareness by means of a song which we sang with great frequency:

> I'm a lover of the Southland
> Living down in Alabam'
> In the fairest of her counties
> In her favored Birmingham!
> Garden spot of dear old Dixie

> She has made me what I am,
> And Birmingham's my home!

By some stroke of rebel genius or, perhaps, defiant mockery, we were taught to sing these words to the tune of the "Battle Hymn of the Republic" ! The song represented an almost militant pride of place and race, and we were singing it long before the Supreme Court decision of 1954 and subsequent events made our city appear reprehensible in the sight of the whole nation and the world. Birmingham's my home. It is the truth and will always be the truth. "No one can efface his origins, the marks of which he carries with him everywhere."

But that theme is only a small part of the story, for there were other songs we were taught to sing, and which we sang with comparable gusto. While in the public school I was being taught to sing of my love for a particular place and a particular people, in the Sunday school of Avondale Methodist Church I was learning John Oxenham's hymn:

> In Christ there is no East or West,
> In him no South or North;
> But one great fellowship of love
> Throughout the whole wide earth.

Lest anyone miss the message, the room in which we met was dominated by a portrait of Jesus surrounded by children of all races.

The story of my life has been decisively influenced by the attempt to live out the implications of the two songs and at times being emotionally torn apart by the resulting tension. In recent years I have been able gradually to recognize that this tension itself has been one of the creative forces in my growth as a person. It is when persons are *not* aware of what is happening inside them, when they are not reconciled to who they are, that the tension may be turned inward in self-destructive ways or vented in an outward assault upon other persons or things.

We never truly know who we are until we have come to terms with who we were. Some deny their past by refusing to acknowledge its true character and in so doing live out on a personal level the axiom that those who are ignorant of history are doomed to keep on repeating it. Others relate to their past by rebelling against it, asserting their present as a *reversal* of their past. This is at best a half-way step toward becoming who you are, for when we try to say who we are by flaunting who we are *not,* we are still bound to the past and therefore still not free.

This is not to say that personal honesty requires us to resign ourselves to the present consequences of past experience. On the contrary, there is a kind of creative remembering which approaches the character of psychotherapy in that it dredges forth that which one has previously blocked from awareness in order that these aspects of the past may be de-activated in terms of whatever unconscious destructive influences they have brought to bear upon us. These dynamics hold true for groups as well as for individuals, a fact which can be amply illustrated by reference to the "consciousness raising" techniques of many newly self-conscious groups in contemporary America.

America the Colorful

Until recent times there were two of almost everything in the South, one for "white" and one for "colored." Looking back, I wonder now which public water fountain would have been chosen by a thirsty Asian and whether or not he would have felt a twinge of caution in either case. Psychologically, at least, this kind of two-way division of the country has not been limited to any one region, for in many statistical measures you are either "white" or "nonwhite." The terminology is racist through and through in that it sets up "white" as the standard from which all others deviate. It is like saying "regular and irregular," or "normal and abnormal."

The chaplain at Mills College, an American of Japanese ancestry, suggests that in fairness we might change the white/nonwhite categories so that in the future we will designate our racial identity as either "colorful" or "colorless." The truth is that people are experiencing a new sense of who they are and where they have come from, and as a society we are groping for a national self-understanding which will express and celebrate our history as a collection of histories, most of which remain substantially untold.

We have attempted to build our society around a single story, the story which has dominated the textbooks in American history. Even so apparently harmless a statement as "Columbus discovered America" presupposes that the story is being told from a European perspective, for the ancestors of Indian children were intimately acquainted with this land thousands of years before Columbus was born. Even the fact that all the native American peoples are called "Indians" obscures their separate stories. When the pilgrims landed at Plymouth Rock, this continent was inhabited by numerous distinct cultures which had existed since antiquity. The Algonquins lived in bark huts on the East Coast, planting corn and foraging through the forests for a livelihood while others, like the Sioux, lived on the Great Plains in tepees made from the hides of buffalo, an animal which they depended upon for survival. The Pueblos of the Southwest built adobe houses several stories high and enjoyed their own distinct cultural heritage. What about the Hopis, Navajos, Cherokees, Creeks, and so on?

I can't recall being taught in the public schools I attended that five thousand Americans of African descent fought in the War for Independence or that more than fifty thousand black men lost their lives with the Union Army in the Civil War. In no literature class was I ever asked to read Richard Wright's novel, *Native Son,* which I now consider an American classic, nor was it ever suggested that virtually all our popular culture has grown from the seedbed of black artistry, as represented by spirituals, the blues, jazz, and the minstrel show. George Washington Carver got into the story for doing so much with the peanut, but when the peanut market brought prosperity to a town whose cotton economy was destroyed by an insect, the citizens gratefully erected a monument to the boll weevil.

The absence of so many stories from the telling of the larger American story is not totally the result of malevolent motives. Had we not adopted *e pluribus unum* as our motto: "from the many, one"? Were we not about the business of creating a new nation in which we would prize only the individual, *regardless* of race, creed, color, or national origin? What must be said, now that we have had two centuries to work under this rubric, is that our vision of what America is and what it might become, as grand as it is, has not been adequate. If, as John F. Kennedy put it, our task is to "make the world safe for diversity," it is a task we must begin at home.

One Nation Under What God?

As the two hundredth birthday of our founding as a sovereign nation approaches, it is time to think about getting on with the American revolution. For more than a decade now it has been all too apparent that the familiar sentiment "Give me your tired, your poor, your huddled masses yearning to be free" is an increasingly ironic invitation, for we have heard from the concrete canyons of our cities, from the sharecropper shacks of our rural South, from the barren reservations of our parched plains, the cries of the tired American poor, themselves yearning to be free. It is not as though the revolution has failed because the present generation has dropped the torch of freedom. Something has been wrong from the very beginning.

We are only now beginning to realize the extent to which the prevailing assumptions of American consciousness have continuously subverted the realization of the full implications of July 4, 1776. One way of getting at what went wrong, and still goes wrong, is to enumerate and bewail "the manifold sins and wickedness" of America. As a matter of fact that is an important thing to do, but by itself it does not help. We must locate the distortions in the collective personality of the nation and make some changes in the way we think and feel if we are ever to be able to change the way we behave.

I believe that the fundamental problem with the American experiment is religious in character. Please note that I did not say that the *answer* to the American dilemma is a religious one. There is not now, nor has there ever been, a shortage of persons vigorously promoting this or that religious answer to all our problems. Paradoxically, perhaps, it is necessary to realize that our *problems* are perpetuated by what are essentially religious assumptions before we can understand how many of the answers we are groping for must also be religious in nature.

An American Indian has written a book called *Custer Died for Your Sins.* The title alone is worth the price of the book to anyone who will take the trouble to reflect upon its implications. Vine Deloria, Jr., describes in this volume the story of the religious aspect of the encounter of the American Indian peoples with the hordes of foreigners who began a massive invasion of their native land a few hundred years ago. The story he tells is prerequisite to any understanding of the contribution religion might make to the continuation of the American Revolution.

During 1860–1880, the United States government confined the native American peoples to reservations as part of its military strategy to "win the West." Ironically, once they were thus carefully confined, they were subjected to decades of programs designed to prepare them for life in white society. A systematic attempt was made to destroy the tribal cultures through the introduction of the government school and the white man's church. Children were separated from their families and forbidden to speak their own language. The practice of tribal religions was prohibited as was just about every other social activity with the exception of Christian worship.

So what is wrong with taking the good news of salvation to people who have not heard it? Although it may appear to be so at first glance, that is not the question which needs to be argued. It is not necessary to impute less than benign motives to those who carried on the missionary programs or to discount whatever humanitarian goals they actually achieved. Deloria's critical point is that the churches collaborated with the government in a largely successful attempt to destroy tribal cultures. In many cases, missionaries appear to have applied the pressure which was the key to the final destruction of an ancient way of life, for only "where Christianity failed, and insofar as it failed, Indians were able to withstand the cultural deluge that threatened to engulf them." [2] The tribes which mustered the will to resist the gospel were able to survive while the others disintegrated.

The assumption that America was destined to be a Christian nation, which was implied by the cooperation of church and state in the evangelization of the reservations, is an unresolved issue which continues to undermine both the goal of religious freedom which was established at the beginning of our national experience and the best interests of the churches themselves. What is the long-range impact upon the country when it is saturated with a "Calling Our Continent to Christ" campaign in the mass media, as was the case in 1973? If one pattern of belief and behavior is set as the ideal standard for all, there can be no real freedom and no genuine democracy. And, to the extent that the churches have allowed themselves to be an instrument of national policy, no matter how noble its intent, they have to that extent sacrificed the possibility of prophetic witness.

Vine Deloria, Jr., is himself an Indian of Christian background and, having attended a seminary with the intention of becoming a minister, is quite well versed in Christian theology and history. But he has found it increasingly difficult to affirm his identity as an Indian and a Christian at the same time. For one thing, the weight of Christian complicity in the destruction of his cultural heritage has become too heavy to bear as the struggle of his people with the state and federal governments has intensified. For another, he feels that the current crisis in American life as manifested in such things as the Indo-China war, the environmental crisis, and the Watergate scandal, to name but a few, has proven the inadequacy of the Christian religion to make an effective contribution to the building of a sane and just society.

This is actually what the death-of-God uproar of a few years ago was all about. The accumulation of destructive behavior—which had the implicit consent of the Christian majority of Americans—had reached the point at which belief in the God proclaimed by the churches was declining as a live option for many. In Deloria's words, "What happened in the last decade is that in all probability the logic of Western culture and the meaning of the Christian world view which supported the institutions of Western culture were outrun by the events of the time." [3]

The only alternative which Deloria sees for America as a whole is to abandon Judaism and Christianity and find new spiritual roots in the native Indian religions. Those who own the land politically will never find peace of soul until they come to reconciliation with those who own the land spiritually. White teen-agers by the thousands have already turned to the reservations in the hope of finding nourishment for a spiritual hunger which apparently could not be satisfied by the religious alternatives available to them in the traditional places. They have decided that God is not dead, he is red!

This latest of Deloria's books, which is actually titled *God Is Red,* is an important analysis of the religious problem in America. But the suggestion that we have available in Indian religions a source of spiritual vitality which can become the true American religion is more a restatement of the problem than a way out of the dilemma. Deloria asks, "Brotherhood of man may be a noble ideal, but can it be achieved in any society that is not homogenous?" [4] When he answers "probably not," it seems to me that his answer to the religious dilemma of America is simply to put the shoe on the other foot. The rest of us must surely ask, "Is *our* cultural and religious heritage worth nothing at all?"

Interestingly, Deloria's solution is not convincing at least partially because he is himself unconvinced. As one reviewer puts it, he is "not yet sure how—or whether—to blot out what he has learned of Christianity, so that what he feels as an Indian can dominate his being." Regardless of what the past holds for each one of us, there are elements of personal history which we have to come to terms with. On one level, that is what Deloria is attempting to work out in his writings, but he is both Indian *and* Christian, and, in my judgment, he ought to work at a creative personal reassessment of the two together. Such is the road which many must take if theological reflection is ever to realize its potential as a transforming and healing resource for American society.

Theology in Black and White

In the San Francisco Bay area, Christians of Asian descent have come together to form the Asian Center for Theology and Strategy. Roy I. Sano, Interim Director of the Center, feels that the "recognition of ethnicity could have considerable impact upon the way we do our theology, or reflect religiously upon our experiences. It could introduce an American phase in theological initiative." [5] Such an affirmation flies in the face of important traditional assumptions by appearing to encourage color consciousness in both the nation and the church. In both settings we like to think of ourselves as color-blind, and to emphasize that the real differences among us are purely individual. Way down deep inside, we are all basically the same. Has it not been the genius of the Christian church, and the American nation as well, to recognize this essential unity of the human race?

Well, yes and no. We are at a point in our history where it is possible and necessary to see that there are blurs in our noblest picture of the future. We are being told now, by those it was our intention to rescue, that the liberal visions of human unity carry the implicit assumption that unity requires unanimity, and that unanimity requires the recognition that *our* way is the authentic, universally human way. This holds true whether we are talking about politics, economics, personal morality, or religion. In terms of our original vision of unity, we have reached the point where we must take what will appear to many as a step backward before we can go forward. We must acknowledge that we are different before we can truly understand how we are the same.

In this spirit, I would like to point out that I am writing, self-consciously, as a white, Anglo-Saxon Protestant. I am doing so for a number of reasons, one being, as I indicated earlier, that I, too, am interested in coming to terms with questions of personal identity and meaning, and that this quest necessarily involves rethinking my Christian heritage, my American citizenship, and my experiences as a white man from Alabama. I also write in this fashion because I think that the emergence of ethnic consciousness in this country cannot realize its potential for transforming our national self-understanding until white Protestants attempt to understand the full implications of the issues involved.

The time for such reassessment of our national experience has never been more urgent than it is at the present moment. The sixties were a time of such strife for the nation that the majority wanted to go into the seventies under the leadership of a national administration which was pledged to "bring us together again." When the Watergate bomb exploded it revealed the fact that our new national consensus had gathered around a central core that turned out to be a moral vacuum. *Now* who are we and where are we going?

I write as I do also because almost all the accusing fingers in recent years have pointed toward the white Protestant community. The assumption has been that we comprise a monolithic, all-powerful group which has consistently divided the spoils of American abundance for the exclusive use of ourselves. For all its obvious relevance, this view obscures the fact that the white Protestant community is itself a rather diverse mixture of groups. Growing up in the South, I was always taught that the people to look out for were fast-talking Yankees, not the blacks, Italians, Syrians, Germans, and others who lived in our community. It is time for a new understanding of who the white Protestants are, for all the newly self-conscious groups in our society "will be frustrated if they wish forever to take for granted the security of the WASP establishment. It cannot serve as everyone's generalized 'other' in the future." [6]

Terms such as "WASP values" and "WASP culture" are freely tossed about as though they refer to concrete realities in the life of a particular community. I want to argue that such terms are used either with an utter lack of precision or they have no meaning at all. Most probably "WASP" has come to mean about the same thing as "the establishment," and if that is the case, it should be recognized that much which ought to be invoked when the word Protestant is used simply does not apply in this connection. The very word itself is incompatible with this application, and if it is not incompatible with this usage, it is clear that the word has become divorced from its history.

Who are the most rootless persons on the American scene today? Is it not the children of white Protestants, drifting about among the various countercultures? They have been taught to despise their own traditions. Look at them as they go casting about for some sort of heritage: Can we learn to groove on black soul? How about entering a cosmic frame of reference through drugs? Or maybe India! Find a guru and follow him forever! Or maybe try the Hopi route, and if that turns into a bummer, drift on down to Mexico in search of Castaneda's Don Juan. And finally, desperately, come as close as we can to our roots while still denying them: turn on to the fundamentalist's Jesus! At least the Book— the words and phrases—are familiar, are somehow *ours*. And if that doesn't work?

The spiritual frustration of the young is a direct outgrowth of the theological bankruptcy of the churches. In my years as a college chaplain, scores of young people have told me that their pastors will discuss anything with them but the life and death issues of personal faith. They did not have to remind me that the same is true of campus ministers, many of whom have been more interested in "relevance" or in finding a nonreligious justification for their jobs, than in dealing with worship and faith.

A few years ago I was invited to offer a study course for church school workers in a large church. In order to focus upon their own perception of their needs, I proposed a list of some twenty questions and asked them to indicate which would be of most immediate concern to them. By far, the dominant concern of this group of church leaders, those with the responsibility for teaching the young, was, What does faith really mean? I have repeated this survey with groups in other churches, and always with the same result. In the pages which follow I hope to shed some light on how this situation has come about and, hopefully, to suggest some basic theological affirmations we can make in beginning to recover our religious roots.

I understand myself to be writing primarily for WASP readers. One of the dominant struggles of my own life has been a quest for meaning which led me at first to reject my past, then to struggle with it, and at last to accept it for what it is: an interesting mixture of the rotten and the ripe. In this process I have become convinced that one does theological reflection in the light of who one *is,* and that creative recall is an indispensable tool in the religious quest. Insofar as we are all members of groups which have great bearing upon our sense of who we are, there is a kind of collective remembering which is also important to the search for a truly personal faith. This is why ethnic theology is important: it helps us to bring the Christian gospel to bear upon real life, upon our own experiences as a particular people. To say that God acts in history, as Christians always have, is to open the possibility of discerning his presence in *personal* history, in the autobiographies of persons and groups.

It follows that I will not presume to write a definitive statement of what faith *must* mean for white Protestants. What I am doing is ethnic theology in the sense that I write with a consciousness of who I am and where I have come from. I hope that in the process of explaining how I have come to be able to make certain faith affirmations I will say something which will be of value to others.

The most powerful theological work which has been done in America in recent years is the black theology developed primarily by James H. Cone. Here is the prime example of theological reflection done in the light of a particular people's history and for the sake of their own liberation. But the implications of Cone's work go far beyond the black community. Because of who I am, it does not seem possible for me to make theological sense of my experience without facing the challenge of black theology.

Once the ethnic issue is raised in theological terms, it is clear that a lot of work must be done in a lot of places at the grass roots level. Although Vine Deloria's red theology is currently moving away from a Christian base, his writings continue to be an important resource for the churches. The Asian Center for Theology and Strategy is in the beginning stages, but holds great promise for the future. Without ignoring these and other important developments, this book will be a kind of theology in black and white. As a white person with deep roots in Alabama soil, the black experience in America has affected me most immediately and most deeply, and it is impossible for me to come to terms with my past without thinking this perspective through.

At the outset, I am concerned that many white Protestants

will view what I am doing as an essentially negative enterprise. Let me assure you that it is not my intention to tear down without building up. In mining for ore it is often necessary to disrupt and displace a familiar landscape—much to our dismay. In this case, I am convinced that there is undiscovered treasure in the Protestant past, and that once we have brought it forth, we will be able to make our contribution to the restoration of a beautiful, colorful America. Between now and then, some blasting and digging are indispensable.

II.
The Selling of the Protestant

The Rise of Protestant Nativism

Throughout most of their history, the Americans have been a "heathen" people. Although there were established churches in most of the original colonies, remarkably few of the colonists showed a personal interest in organized religion. That such was the case during the colonial period is vividly illustrated by the fact that when independence was achieved and church membership placed on a voluntary basis, a very small minority of the population chose to affiliate. During the first few decades of the young nation's life, church members comprised some 4-7 percent of the total population.

Viewed from a broad historical perspective, this situation changed with amazing rapidity. Under the influence of numerous revivals and popular moral crusades in America, more people joined the Christian church during 1800–1960 than in any comparable period in its entire history. During the same years, Roman Catholic and Jewish persons were swelling the United States population through mass migrations from Europe. Thus the religious complexion of the country was radically altered. By 1960, some two-thirds of the American population had affiliated with religious groups, and most of the remaining third thought of themselves as having Protestant, Catholic, or Jewish identity.

29

The colossal expansion of Protestantism into an un-churched population is virtually unique in religious history in that it was accomplished on a free and voluntary basis. Ironically, even those who masterminded the growth of the churches were unaware of the full significance of what they were doing. Rather than glorying in the conquest of a heath-en population, the revivalists themselves promoted the myth that America had strayed from a lost age of faith and needed only to return to the vision of the founders. As Franklin Littell and other historians have shown, the implications of this historically uninformed approach to evangelism were extremely significant.[1]

For one thing, mass conversions on the presupposition of a past Golden Age of faith in a Protestant America led the revivalists to miss the full implications of being a free church, as opposed to a state sanctioned church. Confusing the in-ternal discipline required of a free church with the political enactment available to an established church, the revivalists did not hesitate to seek legislative support for their causes. The various crusades against alcoholic beverages, legal coer-cion of sabbath observance, and the controversy over the teaching of evolution in the schools are good examples of this tendency.

With a few notable exceptions, religious awakenings in America have been associated with popular social movements of one sort or another. Revivalists have so exploited such causes to win converts that the specifically *Christian* signifi-cance of a decision to join a church has often been blurred. Indeed, the ethical and theological substance drained out of revivalism when it was realized that large numbers would join the churches "to affirm a traditional view of America." Thus, internal church discipline gave way to the quest for legislated holiness; membership standards became no more than the mores of society at large.

Littell's chief point in all this is not to lament the "decline" of American Protestantism, but to do just the opposite. He wants to show that the crisis of theological and ethical integrity is an inevitable by-product of winning converts at a rate far in excess of the church's ability to train them in the meaning of faith and the nature of Christian obedience. When it is understood that America was a "heathen" nation at the beginning of the nineteenth century, it can be seen that we share the situation of the younger churches in Asia and Africa today. Converts have been brought into the churches bringing with them their previous beliefs and codes of conduct which have blended with elements of the faith to produce a hybrid religion. The problem is as old as the first-century debate over Gentile converts. Only the vast scale of the dilemma in America is new.

The result of the process described above has been the Americanization of Protestantism to produce the religion of "nativism": an amalgam of Christian doctrines, elements of the Enlightment philosophy espoused by the fathers of the nation, and various beliefs about the origin and destiny of the nation itself. The process of Americanization has also affected Roman Catholics and Jews to such an extent that some students of American culture have spoken of a common religion which is shared by all Americans.

The distinction which is being drawn here is a very difficult one to make, and one which has haunted the church from the very beginning. When the gospel is received by a new constituency, a dynamic interchange occurs. In order to learn any new thing we have to relate it to what we have known previously, and when we relate the new insight to past experience we inevitably alter it to some degree. It is plain to see that the Christian message found expression in new categories of thought when it moved from Jerusalem to Rome and Alexandria. The question which must constantly be raised concerns the extent to which who is affecting whom. In America, the reopening of this question is long overdue.

American Religion: The Sociological Perspective

The blending of Christian belief with the notion that America has a divinely appointed role to play in human history has in recent years attracted the interest of a growing number of sociologists. Assuming the hypothesis that "every society has to an important degree a common religion," Will Herberg identified what he called the American Way of Life as "the operative faith" of the American people. Studying the latest wave of church expansion, which occurred in the 1950s, Herberg concluded that to be a Protestant, Catholic, or Jew are the alternative ways of being an American.[2]

The extent to which the vitality of religious groups in America is a function of their supportive relationship to a more generalized American religiousness is made clearer by the analysis of Robert N. Bellah. His description of a "civil religion" which unites the American people indicates that nativism has matured into a full-blown religious system complete with symbols, rituals, holy days, shrines, saints, and sacred writings.

The chief symbol of the American religion is the flag, and the most familiar ritual is the Pledge of Allegiance to the flag, with related gestures and music. The founding fathers— properly mythologized—serve as saints, and their writings, chiefly the Declaration of Independence and the Constitution along with the speeches made at crucial moments in the nation's history, are sacred scriptures. Although the Lincoln Memorial is the chief shrine to which devotees make pilgrimages, the Tomb of the Unknown Soldier, and more especially, the graves of the Kennedy brothers, rival it in importance.

The most significant celebration of the civil religion is the inauguration of a new president, but Memorial Day is important, as is the ritual behavior associated with Thanksgiving, Independence Day, etc.[3] The basic beliefs of the civil religion center in a confidence in the prominent role of America in the divine plan, which includes God's special sanction of the nation's political and economic institutions. The chief structural support of the civil religion is found in the public school system, where children are first introduced to its symbols and rituals.

Whether one speaks of nativism, or the American Way of Life, or the civil religion, it is clear that the doctrine of the separation of church and state has not prevented the rise of a religious establishment in America. Although church leaders have exploited this native religiousness with remarkable success, they have seldom been aware of the high price involved. But the true nature of the transaction has not been lost to shrewd political leaders who have long assigned the churches a supportive role in relation to established political and economic powers. In a speech to 2,400 Lutheran young people, an attorney general of the state of Arizona said, "In America today we come nearer than ever before in history to rendering unto God the things that are God's when we render unto Caesar." [4]

That remark may be the best possible statement of the dilemma of American Protestantism. But it still presents only half the picture. In recent years, growing numbers of Americans, particularly the young, have found it difficult if not impossible to render unto Caesar. We face the prospect of celebrating the national bicentennial with hundreds, if not thousands, of young Americans exiled to foreign lands for the sake of their consciences. And, as we have described the situation here, such political dissent and disaffection constitute a theological crisis in popular religion. Therefore, those who will not give to Caesar his due receive the harsh treatment normally reserved for blasphemers and heretics.

The Crisis in American Religiousness

In a classic study of the symbolic life of Americans, William Lloyd Warner has given detailed attention to the Memorial Day observances which have traditionally been very important community events in New England. Fused with the theological theme of the sacrifice of the incarnate God, the annual ceremonial remembrance of the death of soldiers provides "powerful sacred symbols which organize, direct and constantly revive the collective ideals of the community and the nation." [5]

For a variety of reasons, but chiefly because of our prolonged involvement in the Indo-China war, the nation has been sinking deeper and deeper into a spiritual malaise which is best understood as a growing crisis of faith at the level of the civil religion. During the war, for example, a crucially important symbol lost its power: as a result of the war in general, and episodes such as the My Lai massacre in particular, the image of the soldier fallen in foreign fields of battle ceased to evoke spontaneous emotions of honor and glory as a patriotic ideal.

This point was dramatically illustrated when the nationally known columnist, Art Hoppe, abruptly abandoned his usual style of humorous satire to confess in sober tones his disillusionment with his country as a result of the war. The shocking realization had suddenly come to him that he was hoping for an American defeat in Southeast Asia. He described the experience as a loss of *faith,* and yearned once again to have faith in the nobility of this country's causes and the justness of its ideals. Needless to say, recent scandals in Washington involving blatant violations of minimum standards of public trust and moralty have compounded this dilemma for millions.

The point here is to understand this crisis of confidence in religious terms, to see it as an undermining of the theological assumptions of the American Way of Life. And, further, to expect that because of the symbiotic relationship between them, a loss of faith in the justness of the nation's causes is bound to have an adverse effect upon the Protestant churches in particular.

In fact, a struggle has been going on within the churches for several years now over their relationship to the civil religion, although it has not been defined as such. The lines of division in the struggle are basically those which Martin E. Marty calls the focal points of a historical polarity within Protestantism: postmillennialism and premillennialism—those who believe that the achievement of universal brotherhood and peace is the goal of history, and those who believe that such will occur only *after* divine intervention brings the present age to a close. The former identify with politically liberal attitudes toward the society while the latter's tendency to expect little from social change pushes them in a politically conservative direction.

The Civil Rights movement, born in the black churches and joined by the liberal churches of the North, made a powerful appeal to native American religiousness in seeking equality for blacks. In time, this appeal was countered by a vigorous thrust from the right wing of Protestantism which seeks to bolster the political status quo through strengthening the identification of the civil religion with the evangelical movement. The nature of the conflict is evident in two sermons preached by Protestant clergymen at the site of the chief shrine of the American Way, the Lincoln Memorial.

In what some regard as the high moment of the Civil Rights movement, some 250,000 persons participated in the

March on Washington in August of 1963. The climax of that day was an address by Dr. Martin Luther King, Jr., at the Lincoln Memorial. In words that are now very familiar to us, Dr. King outlined his dream of a nation ruled by freedom and brotherhood. "I have a dream," he said. "It is a dream deeply rooted in the American dream . . . that one day this nation will rise up and live out the true meaning of its creed, 'We hold these truths to be self-evident: that all men are created equal.' " This powerful appeal to what he understood to be the faith of the founding fathers was capped by an eloquent elaboration of the hymn, "My Country 'Tis of Thee," with repeated emphasis upon the phrase "Let freedom ring!"

Seven years later, on July 4, 1970, another Protestant preacher stood in the same spot and spoke to the thousands of citizens he had invited to join him there for the purpose of "honoring America." In his sermon, Billy Graham said that basic American institutions such as the presidency, congress, the flag, and the home are "under attack." With his usual fervor, he continued, "We are here to say with loud voices that, in spite of their faults, *we believe in these institutions*" [italics added].

Following the sermon, the crowd then marched to the Ellipse, a large area with a commanding view of the White House, and celebrated what must be described as a sacrament. An enormous American flag was raised on a white pole while Boy Scouts distributed miniature flags to the crowd. The participants then filed past to place the smaller flags in a bed of white sand at the base of the large flag pole. When all the smaller flags were in place, they formed the letters "U.S.A." [6]

The two episodes reflect different views in a struggle to define the true nature of the civil religion. Dr. King's interpretation was a broad vision of justice which specifically

included interreligious as well as interracial brotherhood,
and was linked to a program of far-reaching social change.
The implications of his position led him to condemn
United States involvement in Vietnam. While Billy Graham
was careful to include black people, priests, and rabbis in
the "Honor America" program, he clearly has aligned himself on the side of political and economic conservatism. In
spite of repeated warnings on the imminent end of history,
in the tradition of revivalists before him, Graham delights in
the friendship of presidents and in his participation in secular, if not utterly pagan, affairs such as Rose Bowl parades
and popular television programs. He refused to comment
on the morality of the Indo-China war while publicly en-
dorsing President Nixon's policy of Vietnamization.[7]

What is at stake in this struggle on the civil religion level
is an issue which few care to acknowledge openly. It is the
question of the extent to which America is to understand
herself as a Protestant nation with a divinely appointed role
in world affairs. The answer to the question is crucial to
the nation's future. And the source of that answer is in
whether or not Protestantism in this country can find the
resources within itself to define its theological integrity quite
separately from the claims of nationalism.

The Promise in the Present Dilemma

In the space of 160 years the churches moved from a pe-
ripheral role in American society to a prominent position
near the center. In large measure this phenomenal growth
was achieved by identifying the evangelistic impetus with a
series of popular social movements. Two important consequences of this ecclesiastical success have been noted: (1)
the notion of America as having been conceived in the beginning as a white Protestant paradise was implanted in the cul-

tural psyche, and a marked religious flavor permeated public life and (2) the churches paid for the growth and symbiotic relationship to political power at the cost of their own theological and ethical integrity.

In spite of all the diatribes which have been unleashed against the churches in the last decade, it is possible to give a very promising interpretation to the present situation. In keeping with the historical thesis above, it can be said that the perversion of the gospel through the introduction of alien elements is a normal development which was bound to follow upon the heels of so successful a period of converting the "heathen" in massive numbers. By the constant use of such terms as revival and renewal, the churches still assume a past age of faith and therefore promote the sense of failure and frustration characteristic of the present. The tendency is to reach for still another shot of energy from the resources of American native sentiment, but such is a serious misreading of both the past and the present opportunity.

It can be argued that the theological crisis we have heard so much about is, in reality, a crisis for the culture first and for the churches only secondarily. The crux of the religious crisis today is in the civil religion; the young sew flags, not crosses, on the seats of their jeans. It is the native American faith which is faltering, and the churches will suffer theological dissipation only to the extent that they persist in seeking their life force from essentially alien sources.

What is called for now is for the churches to reassess their message and mission in the light of studied judgments about the requirements of faithful obedience to Jesus Christ in this time and place. The present moment cries out for us to ask if the God we worship really *is* active in the affairs of human history. Indeed, merely to face the question seriously may itself be a sign of his nearer approach.

We are not talking about entering a period of withdrawal

and introspection. The challenge before us is the discovery of theological and ethical integrity in the churches at a time when the culture is experiencing spiritual impoverishment and moral frustration. In the nature of the case, "self-analysis and self-discovery in the religious bodies may have . . . considerable value in clarifying some cultural, social and political issues." [8] The first step forward, nevertheless, is the realization that what happens to America cannot be the first concern of the church of Jesus Christ. The national destiny and the progress of the kingdom of God are not— after all—necessarily synonymous. While the kingdoms of this world may someday become the kingdom of our Lord, until such time the latter must have a prior claim upon the churches.

III.
Black Protestants: The Saving Remnant?

The health of American Protestantism is endangered not so much by hardening of the arteries as by a hyperactive thyroid gland; not the problems of old age, but those of growing too much too soon. This does not mean that the future is bright in terms of the criteria of success to which we have become accustomed. Most of the mainline denominations are not growing at a rate in excess of the rate of population growth, once considered an indication of progress, and it would be unrealistic to assume that the financial commitments made during the religious boom will not be continuing problems in the near future. Nevertheless, the basic question facing American Protestantism is that of theological identity, and the prospect of an awakening of vital Christian faith in the churches is a cause for excitement and anticipation, not despair. Rather than lamenting this or that "crisis" we should be asking where we might turn for insight into the meaning of the gospel and the nature of Christian discipleship for our situation.

The Failure of Theologians

The Christian church has survived through the ages on the basis of its ability to adapt—however painfully at times

—to cultural changes. It is the theologian's job to attempt to facilitate this adaptive process. Ideally, he stands at the collision point between the inherited forms of the faith and an ever-changing world, bringing the implications of the gospel to bear upon each new situation.

In this continuing process the interaction is undeniably reciprocal: the Christian witness affects, and is affected by, the changes in its cultural environment. The theological risks inherent in this process of cultural engagement are great, and the assessment of the risks involved forms the primary stimulus of doctrinal debate through the centuries.

In our own time, technological innovation has so increased the rate of social change that theological interpretation has been unable to stay apace. The consequent "meaninglessness" of theological language produced the infamous declaration of "the death of God" by a few American theologians. Whether or not God has recently joined the ranks of the deceased, the difficulty of speaking of the divine ground of human existence must be acknowledged. We are now faced with the question of what sort of theological interpretation of the Christian faith is possible in post–death-of-God America.

In a recent attempt to deal with this question Langdon Gilkey analyzes the current situation by examining contemporary schools of philosophy such as existentialism, linguistic analysis, naturalism, etc. On the basis of these considerations he concludes that the modern mood is one of complete human autonomy, a denial of any sort of ultimate coherence: "Man no longer feels himself to be set within any basic order or context . . . from which he draws not only his being, but also the meanings, standards and values of his life." [1]

The problem with this theological method is that most of us do not derive meaning and value from the musings of professional philosophers or the theologians who occasionally

engage them in debate. This is not to deny either an important place in intellectual history, but simply to recognize—
for good or ill—that it just never occurs to most men to
wonder if the way we find meaning in our lives passes the
test of current canons of philosophical integrity.

One of the reasons why theological language seems to have
lost its vitality is that theologians have in large measure lost
contact with the people who are presumably the intended
benefactors of their interpretations of the faith. Catholic
lay theologian Michael Novak speaks of the need for a theological language capable of speaking in terms of the concrete
present. Such theological work must grow out of "the awareness that our perceptions, our raw, brute experience . . . and
our very fantasies and instincts are given form by subtle
social, political, and economic arrangements." [2] What is
needed today is a theological enterprise which comes into
being out of the engagement of the Christian faith with the
concrete circumstances of human experience.

The Witness of the Black Churches

Any search within the American Protestant community for
the place where the gospel of Jesus Christ has been most consistently engaged with the concrete circumstances of the people in the pews leads inevitably to the black churches. It is
often assumed that Christian categories have been assimi-
lated by black people as a narcotic, lulling them to sleep with
dreams of plenty and rest in heaven, thereby making their
earthly woes bearable. Such has been the hope of those who
oppress them anyway, and no doubt these dynamics have
often been at work. Black theologian James H. Cone himself
dismisses the black church as "not a fit instrument for revolution." But this is by no means an entirely accurate historical generalization.

Church historian Martin Marty writes of the black Protestant that "as a worshipping, suffering, experiencing member of a community he was able to keep alive aspects of Protestant witness which successful and victorious white empire-builders forgot." During the days of slavery, the biblical image of the divine Redeemer who delivers his people from earthly bondage had a powerful influence on black people. Marty describes Nat Turner's rebellion, for example, as an "explicit imitation of Biblical protest and revolt." And David Walker, a black advocate of rebellion in 1828, gave his opinion of the master-slave relationship in these terms: "Have we any other master than Jesus Christ? Is he not their master as well as ours?" [3]

This basic emphasis upon the lordship of Christ as opposed to the claims of the immediate power situation was kept alive when black people began to win their freedom and establish their own churches. The African Methodist Episcopal Church was begun in 1816 under the leadership of Richard Allen, a freed slave who had been trained as an itinerant preacher by Francis Asbury. With the abolition of legal slavery still fifty years away, Allen had the courage to withdraw from the Methodist Church as a protest against racial discrimination at the Lord's table. Perhaps a thorough study of black church history might reveal many examples of theological compromise and a tendency to live at peace with injustice. But that confidence in Christ the redeemer from bondage never died in the black churches was forcefully shown when the Civil Rights movement sprang to life in the 1950s.

So, although black preachers have usually been caricatured by whites, they have maintained a sense of "biblical scope and grandeur sadly lacking in the white churches." While Protestantism as a whole was being sold into its own peculiar bondage to American culture, black Christians did

not forget the God who works in history for the liberation of
his people.

The Challenge of Black Theology

Out of the historical experience of black Christians in
America has come a theological challenge which Protestantism in general cannot afford to ignore. In two books, *Black
Theology and Black Power* and *A Black Theology of Liberation,* James H. Cone has taken the biblical theme of the liberation of oppressed peoples as the starting point for a theological interpretation of the black experience. Themes from
these works will be discussed many times, but at this point
Cone's basic thesis will be described as both an indictment
of, and a challenge to, the white churches.[4]

In the biblical tradition God is known by his mighty acts
in history, and what he does in these events is "always related
to the liberation of the oppressed." God made himself known
"in the history of oppressed Israel and decisively in the Oppressed One, who is Jesus Christ." In the resurrection God
has shown that he is not defeated by oppression, but trans-
forms it into the possibility of freedom. Further, the resurrection of the Oppressed One means that he is present today
in all societies, effecting the liberation of the oppressed. The
task of theology is to point to the contemporary manifestation of God.

For Cone, it follows from the above that to perform the
theological task in America today is to point to the black
revolution as *the* place where God is active and disclosing
himself in our midst: "no theology of the Christian gospel is
possible that ignores the reality of the divine among black
people in this country." Cone does say in his second book
that "blackness" is an ontological symbol which describes
what oppression means in America, i.e., the symbol stands

for the extermination of Indians, the exploitation of Chicanos, etc. But there is no easy escape hatch here for white people who want to qualify as cheaply as possible as "black."

According to black theology the only way to encounter the divine presence is to identify oneself with black people. Echoing Jesus' saying that the only way to save one's life is to lose it for his sake, Cone says that the only way to be free is to become one with those who struggle against their bondage. Although his work is done for the sake of the black community, the implications of Cone's position for white Protestants are both threatening and hopeful. In the long range, when God liberates the oppressed, he liberates the oppressor as well. By refusing to obey the master's rules, the oppressed both free themselves and liberate their oppressors from "enslavement to their own illusions." But white people will miss the real challenge of black theology if they subvert it to their own use without first submitting to the severe indictment it raises against us.

Black Theology and American Religiousness

Of all the critiques of white Protestantism over the last fifteen years, none presents as severe a judgment as that of black theologians:

It is hard to know whether to laugh or weep as the churches make bargains with the principalities and powers: prayers on public occasions, tax exemptions, shying away from vital issues, exhortations to private goodness, promotion of gutless "spirituality," institutional self-glorification—they are all knotted together in a monstrous ungodly tangle that spells death to black humanity.[5]

Cone is unrelenting in his attack upon the religion of the American Way. He denounces the United States Constitution, the Emancipation Proclamation, and all white-controlled political and economic institutions. He has said that Washington, Jefferson, and Lincoln are not heroes for him, and it would be difficult to imagine James Cone using the Lincoln Memorial as a pulpit for any other purpose than denouncing what the shrine itself represents to him. One of his definitions of sin is "believing in the American way of life as defined by its history."

Following Kierkegaard, Cone says that the true prophet must become "anti-Christian" and "unpatriotic." He must challenge "the very existence of the national structure and all of its institutions, especially the established church." To speak of God in this society always forces one to the brink of both heresy and treason. The whole society must be "prophetically condemned." "To be black is to be committed to destroying everything this country loves and adores."

How many white Protestants would be willing to join Cone on these terms? Outside of a few young radicals still within the fold, not very many. But here is one important contribution of black theology to white Protestants: it really *forces* the question of the church's relationship to American society. And if we evade this fundamental issue, the question of discovering theological integrity is decided against us at the start. Can we deny Cone's basic thesis that God reveals himself in his activity in behalf of liberating oppressed peoples? Surely we cannot do so and remain faithful to the biblical witness. If God is active in recent and present American history, at what points might his movement be discerned? Are we moving with him or against him?

In summary, it may be the case that the black churches are the saving remnant in American Protestantism. The answer to this question lies in the response of white Protestants to the theological crystallization of the black experience in the work of James H. Cone. Specifically, he forces us to look for the vital core of contemporary Christian experience by asking where the divine self-disclosure is taking place. By locating the activity of God in a revolutionary challenge to the nation in all its institutional manifestations, the implicit marriage of Protestantism to a native American religiousness is called into question. This is a fortunate development and may become the impetus for self-analysis and theological discovery which the white churches sorely need.

In dealing with such vital issues we are raising the whole question of the relationship between Christ and human culture. That question hovers over everything that has been said to this point, and it must be dealt with more explicitly before the further implications of black theology for white Protestantism can be discussed.

IV.
Black Christ
and
White Culture

The Christ and Culture Problem

In a classic study, H. Richard Niebuhr developed categories for use in defining the various ways the Christian community has chosen to relate itself to its cultural environment. At times, sensitive spirits have felt that obedience to Christ places one in a role of total antagonism to culture, with the only real solution being a withdrawal into one version or another of the Christian commune. At the opposite extreme is the view that Christ and a given culture are in near total agreement; no real conflict is seen between the claims of Christian obedience and the necessity of doing one's civil duties.

In between these extremes are three models which grant the distinction between Christ and culture while at the same time seeking to affirm both. The classic solution of the Middle Ages was to affirm culture, but to set limits upon the possibilities of unaided human achievement. Reason and all other human attainments reach a point at which one can proceed further only on the basis of faith in the Christ who stands *above* culture and alone provides the ultimate value reference for society. A characteristic Lutheran solution to the problem has been to divide the sacred and the secular into two spheres, with the person of faith having to live with the tension created by necessary obedience to both sets of claims. Finally, there is the notion that while Christ and culture are separate, it is the mission of the church to resolve the tension between the two by transforming the culture into the image of Christ.[1]

While these categories are not intended to exhaust the possibilities for a Christian understanding of culture, they do provide helpful tools for understanding the issues involved in the present discussion. Although some case could be made for two or three of these options, we have placed white Protestantism rather squarely in the position of preaching a Christ who is in fundamental agreement with American culture. We have argued that this marriage may be on the rocks, due as much to a crisis in the ideals of the culture as to any discomfort with the arrangement on the part of the churches. And we have said that the crisis presents Protestantism with a good opportunity to set its theological house in order.

In proposing the stance of black theology as a challenge to white Protestantism, it would seem that an unbearable polarity has been set up. On the basis of what has been said so far, Cone is clearly in the "Christ against culture" camp. In addition to all that we said previously with regard to his attack upon American culture, Cone says, "Creative theological reflection about God and his movement in the world is possible only when one frees himself from the powers that be. The mind must be freed from the values of the oppressive society." But almost immediately he continues, "Culture—that is, the situation of modern man—must be the point of departure of relevant theology." [2]

This apparent tension is resolved by the way in which the Christology of black theology is developed. Cone's approach is basically Barthian, issuing in a vigorous *no!* to white culture, spoken from an uncompromisingly Christocentric position. His confidence is in the righteousness of God rather than in the capability of man; Cone does not stand in the tradition of theological liberalism as so many black leaders have. Therefore the persistence of war, poverty, and oppression does not drive him to despair, but to hope in the promises of God's righteousness and to impatience with the way things are in the light of the way God wills them to be.

In the nature of the case at hand, God is seen as acting through the identification of Christ with the liberation struggle of black people. The black revolution *is* the mode of divine self-disclosure to this generation. And, in the Bible, God acts in the history of a particular *community,* not merely in the biographies of individuals. To say that the contemporary manifestation of Christ is appearing within the black community is to make a Christological affirmation which carries with it a cultural component. Cone is really saying something that does not fit easily in Niebuhr's categories: Christ is in opposition to a total culture by means of his identification with a subculture within the larger whole.

Pushed far enough, however, Cone's position would have to be placed in the "Christ the transformer of culture" school. He nowhere indicates an interest in a total *withdrawal* of black people from the American social framework. Although he would probably resist this interpretation as a weakening of his uncompromising opposition to white-dominated structures, to speak of liberation—with reference to political and economic conditions—itself implies an affirmation of the possibilities of culture. That is, people cannot be liberated *from* culture without being liberated *for* some cultural alternative unless withdrawal or the imminent end of history is anticipated. It must be assumed that Cone envisions an America *transformed* by the liberating activity of Christ.

It could be protested that transformation implies the con-

tinuation of present structures in a reformed condition, and
that the proper word is not "transformation," but "revolution." Indeed, some may envision nothing beyond the destruction of the present system; in which case, perhaps, liberation does *not* imply a future in any concrete sense of expectation. The weakness of this particular understanding of revolution will be dealt with below. In forcing the transformation category at this point, the idea is to suggest that black
theology and white Protestantism are not necessarily at opposite ends of Niebuhr's continuum and that white Protestants
may find their identity in relation to a theology of social
change which would at minimum be complementary to the
long-range goals of black theology.

In terms of these categories, what is being suggested for
white Protestants is, first of all, a disavowal of the notion
that we render unto God what is God's when we render unto
Caesar. During one siege of civil turmoil in Birmingham, an
urgent call went out on radio and television for all clergymen to report to the municipal auditorium. When we got
there we were told by the chief of police and by the county
sheriff that we could play an important role in the crisis by
appealing from our pulpits for order and restraint. It seemed
to me at the time that many left that session with a new
sense of importance: there was a major problem here, and
they turned to *us* for help! Nevertheless, that event was the
most overt example of the churches' subservience to principalities and powers that I have experienced. This is not to
suggest that we should have called for chaos and rioting in
order to demonstrate our independence from government,
but to suggest that the relationship between Christ and culture was taken for granted: the proper response of Christians
was to obey those civil authorities whose power was most
immediately at hand.

Again, the vigor with which the war in Southeast Asia

was supported for so long by so many gave ample evidence
that the inclination to have no king but Caesar was not
limited to the Deep South. What I am suggesting is that
the ultimate disillusionment with the war and the subsequent moral collapse of the national administration not only
provide an opportunity to raise these issues, but, in fact,
force them upon us. Many are rushing into the spiritual
vacuum, as always, crying "Christ is the answer." My plea
to white Protestants is that, for once, we squarely confront
Christ as the *question* which is before us.

Harold Cruse: Rebellion or Revolution

To bring the argument up to the present point, we have
said that black theology offers an indictment of white Protestantism as an ally of cultural arrangements which serve to
keep black people in an oppressed condition. We have more
or less accepted the charge while pleading the extenuating
circumstance of a phenomenal growth which made the integrity of our theological stance impossible to maintain. Now
we have been gradually suggesting that the white churches
are not necessarily diametrically opposed to a theological
emphasis which equates the Gospel with the liberation of oppressed peoples.

At this point it should be emphasized that it is not the
prerogative of white people to tell black theologians what
must be meant by their terminology, or to instruct them in
the social implications of their position. Nor do we seek some
way of taming Cone's black Christ in order to link him with a
program of social change which might be manageable for
white churches as presently constituted. It is simply that the
theological vitality is gone from American Protestantism, and
Cone's proclamation that God is revealing himself in con-

temporary movements of liberation must therefore be taken seriously.

However, as we have indicated earlier, white Protestants have a history of attaching themselves to social movements and getting a free ride until the movements run out of steam. At the present time we are writing theological versions of every new cause from what to do about hunger to finding a new appreciation of human sensuality. We need to remember the biblical injunction to "test the spirits to see whether they be of God," for not every spirit blowing in the winds of revolutionary rhetoric may signal the presence of the Redeemer. Not everyone who shouts "Revolution!" may be contributing to the liberation of the oppressed.

The work of black intellectual Harold Cruse is enormously instructive at this point.[3] Cruse acknowledges that the liberation of black people in this country requires a realignment of power relationships so basic and far reaching as to be described as revolutionary, and the present era is replete with examples of oppressed peoples who have thrown off the yoke of colonial masters to achieve the right to preside over their own national development. But it is the implied appeal to the colonial model, when speaking of the black revolution in America, that Cruse calls into question.

There is a fundamental difference between the revolutions of underdeveloped countries against foreign domination and the possibility of a revolution by black people in this country. A revolution is possible in the former case precisely because the societies involved *are* underdeveloped. By overthrowing the alien intruders, a new nation may win the right to develop its own natural resources into an industrial economy within whatever political framework it chooses.

But the black American exists *within* the most highly developed technological society known to history. In biblical idiom, he is *in* the advanced industrial world, but not fully *of* it. Revolution in the sense of an indigenous group winning the right to determine its own economic development is clearly out of the question. Further, even the classical Marxist revolt of workers against capitalist owners is an option whose time has long since come and gone in this society. This is true not only because fewer and fewer workers are needed in production roles, but also because a strong alliance exists between capital and organized labor. Under these conditions, "all purely economic and political reorganizations of any type . . . can be only reformist movements." The goals of the black revolution must be different from those of any colonial predecessor *in order to be revolutionary*.

What is needed in the present cultural impasse is a fresh understanding of what social revolution might mean in this time and place. Several years ago, Cruse argued that the black revolution was stymied because it lacked intellectual leadership which could accurately assess the social reality of modern America and the black man's relation to it. The black leadership which emerged after World War II came from the middle class, a group which was out of touch with black reality at the grass roots, ghetto level. The more recent surfacing of the Black Power movement, although much more radical in posture, also failed to understand the requirements of social revolution in an advanced industrial society. Cruse goes to Albert Camus, himself no stranger to revolutionary struggle, to develop a distinction between rebellion and revolution. Rebellion is an action which is taken largely without a comprehensive strategy, an unreasoned protest, while revolution is an "attempt to shape actions to ideas, to fit the world into a theoretic frame." Much which has been done in the name of the black revolution Cruse would classify as rebellion: "The revolutionary anarchism of urban uprisings always ends up by demanding more state aid from the capitalistic-welfare state apparatus." Too often, black activists have failed to "connect their ideas to the appropriate kind of social actions."

With this kind of critique, Cruse is setting the stage for the presentation of an alternative means of linking ideas to actions which may be more successful in producing revolutionary change. Our hope is that Cruse's analysis may be helpful in the theological task of discriminating among the spirits at work in the world in the hope of discerning the movement of that Spirit whose work always means the liberation of the oppressed.

The Revolution of Consciousness

Since it is clearly impossible for black people to mount a frontal assault upon the system of corporate capitalism at the level where basic commodities are produced, Cruse suggests a black revolutionary thrust at the weakest link in the production chain. This he locates at the point where no tangible goods are produced: the cultural apparatus. It is the cultural dimension of American life that is most vulnerable to fresh ideas, and new ideas are the meat of social revolution. Whoever controls the cultural apparatus "also controls the destiny of the United States and everything in it."

So Cruse advances the concept of "cultural revolution," by which he means "an ideological and organizational approach to American social change by revolutionizing the administration, the organization, the functioning, and the social purpose of the entire American apparatus of cultural communication and placing it under public ownership." Cruse is convinced that this concept can provide the "theoretic frame" which would unite the disparate trends within the black movement and also work toward the alteration of all basic institutional arrangements. The extreme sensitivity of political and economic interests to developments in the communications media indicates that Cruse is indeed probing a very vulnerable area of the social establishment.

The consequences of controlling the image-making capacity of the media are crucial to the maintenance of the present order of social reality, and no revolutionary movement can succeed without coming to terms with this fact. But the weakness in Cruse's position is his failure to show how one goes about getting control of the "cultural apparatus." This aspect of cultural revolution is not clear. But the strength in Cruse is his recognition that lasting change depends upon the alteration of the view men have of social reality, upon a revolution in human consciousness.

At this point, the Cruse argument is joined by a growing company of witnesses. A biographer quotes the late Martin Luther King, Jr., for example, as saying, "For years I labored with the idea of reforming the existing institutions of the society, a little change here, a little change there. Now I feel quite differently. I think you've got to have a reconstruction of the entire society, a revolution of values." [4] Saying that it is futile to concentrate solely on over-throwing governments and economic systems, Theodore Roszak believes that the history of revolution teaches us that "it is the foundations of the edifice that must be sought. And those foundations lie among the ruins of the visionary imagination." The real issue is "altering the total cultural context within which our daily politics take place." [5] Charles A. Reich agrees: "Social change cannot be accomplished without the support of an appropriate consciousness in the people." [6]

It is also interesting to note that a white social analyst has observed the activities of young white radicals and reached conclusions which are very close to those of Harold Cruse. Philip Slater says that the problem with radicals is that they have no truly modern theory of revolutionary change. He urges them to reflect more on their admittedly skillful exploitation of the media and to realize that revolutionary change in this society may not even require altering the basic formal structures of government. Slater does not ask for an end to radical challenges to the structures of power, but for the recognition that change must occur also at the level of motivational forces.[7] It would seem that Cruse's interpretation of revolution in a technologically advanced society is gaining broad intellectual support.

Before considering the sort of change Cruse would like to effect in the self-understanding of America, we might note the religious implications which are appearing at this stage of the discussion. Insofar as a major component of social revolution is a change in "the sense men have of reality," the revolutionary potential of theological thinking would seem to be great. That Christ is at work among black people, leading them to affirm their blackness against a social order which recognizes virtue only in terms of distinctly white values makes plenty of theological sense. The larger implications of the black Christ's movement to destroy/transform the total white-dominated culture remain to be discussed.

V.
Ethnic Pluralism and a New White Consciousness

The Myth of the Melting Pot

In the early years of the colonization of North America, several nations were involved. It was not until the French and Indian War just after the middle of the eighteenth century that British predominance in that portion of the continent which was to become modern America was assured. The conclusion of that war opened the way for pioneers from the British colonies in the East to continue their westward migration into the region of the upper Ohio River valley. Ironically, it was partially the stresses and strains of successful empire building that provoked a revolt in the American colonies and rendered the mother country unable to suppress it.

Although it seems painfully obvious, it is important to remember that those who wrote the charter documents and established the basic institutional structures of the new nation were for the most part "Anglo-Saxons" in lineage and at least nominally Protestant. Catholics, Quakers, blacks, and others had been present for nearly two centuries, and the native Americans—"Indians"—for vastly much longer. But what we often fail to realize is that, for all their vaunted humanitarian sentiments about freedom, dignity, and equality, the Declaration of Independence and the United States Constitution were written with white people in mind.

Indians were not granted citizenship, and the institution of black enslavement was extended.

Basic to Harold Cruse's call for cultural revolution is his claim that in spite of all that has happened since the beginning—emancipation, Bill of Rights, etc.—the fundamental dilemma which was created at the first has not been resolved. In spite of the huge waves of immigration from various parts of the world, the concept of the ideal American as a white, Anglo-Saxon Protestant continues to inform the national consciousness. The melting pot image is a myth which has served only to continue the illusion, since no one is truly let out of that cauldron until he is blanched white—at least psychologically. As one researcher has put it, "For most of American history, only white Protestant needs and interests have been publicly recognized as legitimate." [1]

Cruse argues that the present United States Constitution is inadequate because it nowhere speaks of the rights of *groups,* as opposed to the rights of individuals. This is so, he says, because only the rights of a particular group were even imagined. The Constitution, then, is not in accord with social reality: this is a nation of *nations,* a constellation of ethnic groups seeking power and recognition. Vine Deloria, Jr., points out that the three basic minority groups (blacks, Indians, and Chicanos) were all granted their full citizenship status *as groups,* and argues for an extension of this recognition in other ways. In spite of the cruel treatment of Indians in most matters, Deloria believes that what tribal sovereignty remains to them might become some kind of model for the constitutional rights of groups.[2]

The Reality of Ethnic Pluralism

What is needed in America is the realization that this is an *ethnically pluralistic* society. One ethnic group came to power as the history of the land unfolded, and it has dominated the social system ever since, granting full benefits only to those who in one way or another could prove themselves "white." Now, the dominant white group, while recognizing the many problems which exist, does not recognize that there is any weakness in the core patriotic myths and values. It rarely occurs to us to wonder how sensitive Indians and blacks might feel about singing, "Land where my fathers died,/ Land of the pilgrims' pride." Regardless of what all the "sacred" documents may say, can we really expect the black, red, and brown Americans—and the yellow ones in the wake of the domestic concentration camps of World War II—to affirm enthusiastically that "our fathers brought forth on this continent a new nation, conceived in Liberty, and dedicated to the proposition that all men are created equal"?

Throughout our history, the fundamental decisions affecting the lives of all Americans have been made by white Protestant interests whose power is derived not from inherent superiority or popular consent, but from an early turn of events which gave them the power to establish the rules of the game at the beginning. That the United States government has nearly always acted, and continues to act, on the assumption that the public interest and white self-interest are the same could be illustrated over and again.

In 1887, for example, the United States Congress revoked solemn treaties by breaking up many Indian reservations into small parcels of land which were distributed to individual Indians. The assumption which justified the action was that any able-bodied man with 40 acres and a mule ought to be self-sustaining. This attitude ignored the ethnic reality that the Indians had no tradition of private land ownership, and that many had no skills or interest in farming. But the "public interest" was served in enabling white entrepreneurs to take nine million acres of reservation land for their own use over the following half-century.

The disregard of the interests of the native American peoples by public officials continues to be commonplace. In the 1960s a dam was built across the Allegheny River in New York which flooded the sacred burial grounds of the Senecas even though they had hired their own engineers and proposed a suitable alternative site for the dam. Deloria has written that "more damage is being done to Indian people today by the U.S. Government than was done in the last century." [3] Why? He says, "The primary obstacle at present is the unwillingness or inability of the peoples of Western European descent to give up the idea that we are all the same." [4]

The failure of even our most liberal humanitarian efforts toward helping people is attributable to the basic incongruity between the national self-understanding and social reality. Without a basic recognition of ethnic pluralism our most well-meaning reform programs cannot often succeed. If Cruse is right, the solution to many of these problems lies in precisely the *opposite* direction from that we have so long assumed.

Toward a New White Consciousness

Speaking to the need for an awareness of ethnic pluralism, Robert W. Terry writes,

> The upheavals presently occurring in American society can be interpreted as the creative struggle for pluralism. . . . Everyone loses when there is one definition of an American. . . . Pluralism affirms ethnic variety, a variety that enriches all groups and traditions.

> If we seriously want to eliminate racial injustice in America, instead of pretending to ignore color we must be color-conscious in a radically new way. [5]

The new militancy among minority groups in America is
rooted in a new ethnic consciousness which forces the recognition that we are not all the same. What is lacking is an important key to the achievement of genuine ethnic pluralism:
the realization that white Protestants are themselves an ethnic
presence, one among many ethnic subdivisions of the larger
whole. The fulfillment of cultural revolution depends upon
the realization of *a new white consciousness.*

In familiar terms, there must be an alternative to integration or segregation as modes of dealing with the ethnic variety of the American people. Let us hope that the sordid story
of racial segregation in America is forever a thing of the past.
But let us also recognize that integration, for all its noble
achievements, is not enough. For the most part integration
has been predicated on the assumption that everyone, if given
the opportunity, could find a comfortable place in white-
dominated institutions. The rise of the new ethnic consciousness has been, basically, a reaction to this assumption.

Is it not possible to find the ethnic variety of America an
occasion for celebration? There will be those who charge
that the emergence of color consciousness is a step in the
direction of resegregation, and, understandably, this fear
will be most acute among those minority persons who have
somehow been successful under the present system. But all
I am asking for is a sensitivity which will take the reality of
ethnic pluralism as a presupposition for thought and action
in the quest for freedom and justice.

The exact nature of the concrete changes to be made in
the interests of a just distribution of economic and political
power in America, and the precise character of the programs
to be pursued are not clear. The burden of the argument
being presented here rests on the assumption that it is vain
to push programs of revolutionary structural change in the
absence of serious efforts to facilitate and interpret the revolu-

tionary changes in consciousness which are in fact already under way in some quarters of the society. It is even more vain to promote disruption in the present order, such as it is, with no goals of any sort in view toward which such actions might lead.

But it should be abundantly clear that we are talking about *power*: the power to participate effectively in the decisions which shape the conditions of personal and social existence. Somehow, the distribution of power, both economic and political, must be made responsive to the diversity of ethnic interests. In the kind of democratic republic we have, the people theoretically participate in government by means of elected representatives, and in the popular understanding all any individual needs is the right to vote. But we have, in fact, long recognized that this alone is not enough. By guaranteeing to each state equal representation in the United States Senate regardless of population size, Delaware is as powerful as California in that forum.

Furthermore, it is now painfully apparent that there is another kind of group participation in the political process: the special-interest lobbies in Washington influence decision making to such a powerful extent that they have been called the fourth branch of government. Through campaign contributions, and who knows what else, these powerful interests influence the elective process as well as legislation. The influence of groups is basic to the present political process. Why not redress the power imbalance by extending the principle to include the right of ethnic communities to similar representation? Many decisions, such as the fate of the Indian reservations, affect particular groups far more than the population as a whole. Without numbers and without wealth, the tribes have been at the mercy of government whim.

Anyway, regardless of what the practical consequences must be, the key to meaningful progress in the transition from the present situation to genuine ethnic pluralism seems to rest with the white Protestant group, since—for the historical reasons outlined above—it currently controls all national decision-making structures. Under ordinary circumstances it would be ridiculous to think that a powerful group in control of a society might somehow surrender that dominance to any force other than superior military might. These are not ordinary times, however. American culture faces a crisis which in many ways threatens its future even more ominously than the Civil War did, basically because the society itself is so vastly increased in complexity. A disaffection from the very goals of the society is pervasive, and confidence in the efficacy of established procedures for solving problems is at a very low ebb. It may be that the sharing of the dominant group's powers will be the only way to deal with the present crisis, short of resorting to a cruelly repressive police state in which few, if any, could truly enjoy their lives.

To put the argument in focus once more, what the nation needs at a fundamental level is a change in self-understanding which would affirm the reality that this is an ethnically pluralistic society, a nation of nations. A new ethnic consciousness is already evident within several groups, the blacks most notably. What is needed is the realization by the dominant group that it is also one among many ethnic presences in the nation rather than the colorless, ideal standard for all. Given a Christian commitment to the transformation of culture, the question at issue is the extent to which theological work might be done with special sensitivity to the condition of particular ethnic communities. We have the example of black theology. Does it make sense to think in terms of a *white* theology relating itself to the emergence of a new white consciousness?

VI.
Ethnic Theology and White Liberation

The Genius of Ethnic Theology

For some years now, the notion that theological thinking is by nature *contextual* has been recognized and accepted by many. Even the monumental work of a Karl Barth—while timeless in its overall impact—takes shape in response to contemporary cultural conditions. A theological response which is essentially a condemnation of culture, as Barth's was in the beginning, is nevertheless culturally motivated. It was the emergence of the demonic capabilities of human self-confidence in early twentieth century Europe which evoked Barth's denunciation. While his work stands as a permanent rebuke to all who would identify the kingdom of God with the ambitions of men, it is nevertheless a model of theological sensitivity to current events.

The mistake which has often been made is that while theological systems arise to meet the needs of a particular time and place, this fact has often been missed by those who affirm some new interpretation of the faith. Problems develop in two dimensions, those of time and space. On the one hand, we tend to cling to theological affirmations long after their timeliness has passed. Hence such controversies as those which locked churchmen in conflict with the advancement of scientific knowledge. On the other hand a problem less often

recognized is the folly of attempting to convert persons of
other cultures on the basis of a gospel which carries with it
the prerequisite of adopting alien cultural values. The history of Christian missionary activity is a long story of "cir-
cumcising gentiles": that is, the deculturation of American
Indians, Africans, Asians, etc., in the process of sharing the
Christian faith with them. The resulting damage to the psychological and social health of the "heathen" has done
much to discredit the gospel in the minds of sensitive men
and women everywhere.

It is to this latter problem that the concept of ethnic theology speaks most directly. It attempts to understand the gospel of Jesus Christ in the light of the concrete social situation
of a particular group of people. This means that James H.
Cone is not attempting to work out a theological system
designed to answer unresolved questions about the nature of
the universe, nor is he attempting to provide Christian
answers to philosophical debates. Rather, he is searching for
the reality of God in the midst of the peculiar circumstances
of black people in America. The result is not the appropria-
tion of the gospel as a tool to be used for merely human designs, although the danger is clearly present. The result is a
powerful proclamation of Jesus Christ that says of him that
"he is who he was." That is, the God who made himself
known through the deliverance of Israel from Egyptian
bondage and who made himself known decisively in the
death and resurrection of the Oppressed One from Nazareth
is making himself known in the here and now of American
life in his activity in behalf of the liberation of black people.

The gospel is not good news merely in its *yes* to individual
men, but also in its *yes* to human communities. The real
sense of such a statement may not be clear to white Americans, but a black man can truly be "redeemed" only when
he knows that his blackness is acceptable to God, for his

blackness is an essential component of his being-in-the-world. This is the genius of ethnic theology; it opens up to humanity dimensions of the divine *yes* which have been perceived in modern times very dimly if at all. It is the tragedy of white evangelism that it has held out the promise of no racial distinctions in heaven, for in doing so, it has withheld the divine *yes* to blackness. And in so doing, we have stunted the power of the gospel we proclaim to liberate all men everywhere, ourselves not least of all.

Releasing the vitality so long stored in these deeper implications of the gospel is the gift of black theology to the white churches of America. To be sure, it is a gift which comes wrapped in a judgment against us that is unrelenting in its wrath. It is the gift of one who offers us our very life—in return for our losing it. Cone says, "No white theologian has taken the oppression of black people as a point of departure for analyzing the meaning of the gospel today." But this is precisely the task laid out for us now.

Oddly, to view the gospel in terms of the oppression of blacks forces white people in the direction of a new sense of their own collective existence. Our individualism has often allowed us each to escape responsibility for the collective and cumulative sins which have turned whiteness into a global symbol of exploitation. No white man can truly be free who has not come to terms with the burden of his whiteness. Black theology calls the white Protestant community in particular to the bar of judgment. And that summons is an appointment with reality which none of us can finally escape.

To pick up a theme from the beginning, the turn of events being described here brings within it a note of profound hopefulness. For not only must we confront the shattering of some precious illusions about ourselves, but we will have the opportunity to ask in a truly fresh way what the gospel of Jesus Christ might mean for white Americans in the present dilemma. That is, we will be free to inquire after the liberating presence of Christ *within* the camp of the "oppressor" himself. And should we discover the divine self-disclosure taking place in *our* midst, the problem of theological and ethical integrity in the churches would begin to take care of itself.

Locating the Divine Self-Disclosure

The hallmark of biblical faith is the claim that God is active within the affairs of human history. Certain events have been seen by men and women of faith as pivotal moments in the whole drama of divine human interaction. Almost all of the Old Testament revolves around a few such events, with the chief one being the exodus of the Hebrew people from bondage in Egypt. Whatever the concrete circumstances of that episode might have been, it has been remembered in faith as a mighty act of God: the salvation of a particular people which has had momentous consequences for all subsequent history, especially that of the Western nations.

No one would want to deny that the entire New Testament hangs together around the proclamation of the death and resurrection of Jesus Christ. Again, the details of what actually happened on the occasion in question will no doubt be debated forever. But regardless of how that debate goes, the course of Western civilization has been indelibly marked by the conviction that what happened in and around Jerusalem in those days was a direct result of divine activity. In the circumstances of the life, death, and resurrection of Jesus, God has disclosed his own nature and somehow given his own life to the world.

This understanding of God's activity in history is loaded with many dangerous implications, the most dreadful consequence being the frequent assumption that a particular nation or religious group has been granted a franchise upon the dispensation of the will of God. We have seen how parallels have often been drawn between biblical history and American history, with the Pilgrims being compared to the Hebrew tribes and Lincoln's life and death given a redemptive significance after the order of Christ's sacrificial offering of himself at Calvary. Such notions as "manifest destiny" have continued this basic assumption that the creation and preservation of the American nation has been for the express purpose of providing the agency through which the divine will could work itself out in the world.

In rejecting this tendency of the Protestant side of our heritage to identify the kingdom of God with America, it is not necessary to dispense with the whole notion of God's self-disclosure in human events. What is needed is a reaffirmation of the biblical claims concerning the nature of God's action in the world. We have seen how James H. Cone has done this in pointing to the liberation of oppressed peoples as the mode of God's presence in human events. To locate the divine activity in the present moment, one's attention must be directed to those points where movements for human liberation are taking shape.

On one level this point of view may be seen as just the latest version of the tendency we have deplored, since it locates the action of God with particular groups, i.e., oppressed peoples, and thereby runs the risk of repeating all the old mistakes as liberation becomes a reality. The problem with this criticism, however, is that it is not the place of those with power to caution the powerless concerning the abuses of power. The question for white, Anglo-Saxon Protestants, as the dominant group in American society, is to come to terms with the claim that God is active in movements for human liberation by reflecting upon our *own* experience.

In the first instance, this requires us to acknowledge the claim of liberation theologies that the current of God's movement in contemporary history is running *against* us. To be sure, God's judgment must always be understood in a dialectical fashion: he utters his *no* to man in order to bring him at last to a full realization of the divine *yes* to the whole of humanity. But there is no way to short-circuit this process by assuming the automatic operation of divine grace. Indeed, one of our fundamental religious difficulties is that we have been so presumptuous of God's favor and forgiveness as to empty the notion of transgression of all significance.

Basic to the self-understanding of white Protestant Americans is the notion that we are a fundamentally innocent and good people. President Eisenhower expressed this feeling when he said, "America is great because she is good." This pervasive presumption of innocence will not permit us to come to terms with that aspect of our national character which allows us, even somehow motivates us, to inflict upon mankind unspeakable horrors. We have made repeated references to the extermination of Indians and the exploitation of black people which continue to be present realities in America. While the majority of Americans finally became disillusioned with the war in Indo-China, most Americans, as though perpetuating a tradition of the suspension of belief, have never faced the stark reality of what happened there.

War is generally understood as a necessary evil in which the moral sanctions normally invoked to judge behavior are at least partially suspended. The use of atomic bombs in Hiroshima and Nagasaki, for example, is justified as a decision which was made under extraordinary circumstances in the belief that fewer lives would be lost in the long run if such devices were used to end the war. Without arguing the merits of the decision itself, it is fair to ask if the Ameri-

can people have ever truly understood the human consequences of that decision. In 1970, for example, a quarter-
century after the event, nearly 50,000 persons received treatment and 70 persons died as a direct result of the bomb
dropped on Hiroshima.[1] Reports on the kinds of devices
"tested" in Indo-China further indicate that we possess a
willingness to destroy human life—for whatever military
rationale—by means so extraordinarily cruel as to raise serious questions about our sanity as a people.

One of the characters in Richard Wright's novel, *Native
Son,* says that men will do almost anything to avoid accept-
ing the charge that they are guilty of wrong. When attempts
to justify themselves fail, and "seeing no immediate solution
that will set things right without too much cost to their lives
and property, they will kill that which evoked in them the
condemning sense of guilt." Perhaps the explanation of our
willingness to inflict terrible suffering on others might be
found in such dynamics. The intensity of our present national travail might also be accounted for by the mounting evidence that our cause in Southeast Asia was not just, and our
commitment to social justice at home is not real.

This is not to say that the white citizen *feels* guilty. It is
rather to suggest that we are in fact guilty in the objective
sense of sharing the corporate sins of white America against
nonwhite peoples at home and abroad. And to argue that the
psychic cost to *ourselves* of this unacknowledged guilt—while
not to be lightly compared to the suffering of our victims—
has been, and continues to be, incalculably great. We have
no meaningful future as a people until we come to terms
with our own guilt.

But this is the point at which a critically important distinction needs to be made. When the reality of white guilt begins
to emerge at the edges of our consciousness, we quickly resort
to *doing* something about it. Traditionally, our attempts to

atone for our own vague sense of guilt have taken the form
of a paternalistic posture toward those we have abused, resulting in further compounding their problems. Only one example might be the current horrors of our system of criminal
justice, many of which are a direct result of reform efforts
hailed as highly progressive innovations when first introduced. Another example, already mentioned, would be the
assimilation programs on the Indian reservations.

What is needed now are not new programs of bureaucratic
atonement whereby we try to work out our own salvation in
a way that will guarantee our continued domination of the
structures of power. What is needed now is an openness to
the judgment of God, as made manifest in the emergence of
oppressed peoples, that will lead us toward an honest recognition of divine initiatives in current history. As white
Americans we must assume the uncustomary posture of
looking and listening before we leap. It is only by hearing
the voice of God in the cries of the powerless that we will
acquire the sensitivity to recognize deep within the aching
void which is at the heart of the white Protestant experience today, our own yearning to be united, shoulder to
shoulder, with all who dream of a world in which justice and
peace are sovereign.

In summary, if there is to be an ethnic theology of white
liberation, the first issue it must come to terms with is the
pervasive guilt of white society. Malcolm X began his upward
climb from a life of drug addiction and crime when, in a
prison cell, he came to the insight that "only guilt admitted
accepts the truth." Through its partnership with the civil
religion, white Protestantism has conspired to perpetuate the
lie of American innocence. The road to theological integrity
for the white churches and the path of salvation for the nation lead in the same direction: toward that admission of
guilt which alone makes the recognition of truth possible. We

might begin the painful journey with the assurance that knowing the truth is said to set men free.

Openings for a Theology of White Liberation

God's activity in the liberation of oppressed peoples is surely present in the revolutionary struggle of black Americans against white domination. This is the central affirmation which energizes black theology, and it is crucially important to note that without a similar acknowledgment no theology of white liberation would be possible. God is active in the black revolution in bringing liberation to all men, including white oppressors. The only way for white men to be free is for them to take the side of the oppressed in their struggle against exploitation. The liberation of black people is the touchstone of theological reflection in America today.

This does not mean, however, that white people should try to identify formally with black organizations which are working for liberation. The picture of "radical chic" which Tom Wolfe has drawn in his description of the brief flirtation of New York socialities with the Black Panthers is a painfully realistic look at the way such alliances have often gone.[2] It is not as easy as all that to deal with the burden of whiteness. To identify oneself with this or that movement aimed at racial integration was a noble, and often heroic, act in the recent past. But now the revolution is broader in scope: it aims not at inclusion in the present order, but at the creation of a new order in which blackness is given its due. It aims at the creation of an ethnically pluralistic society in which diversity is welcomed and encouraged. It is the task of white Protestants in particular to get ready for that day by getting *themselves* together, and by discovering the meaning of Jesus Christ for white people today.

This is why we must acknowledge the reality of white guilt,

but not get mired in it. We look at the question of guilt for
the purpose of getting an accurate reading of the factors we
must deal with in the present situation. The future would
be bleak indeed for both America and the world if we could
only describe the dimensions of the demonic side of history
without seeing any possibility of getting beyond the legacy
of past sins. A theology of white liberation must move quickly to the task of locating those points in our own situation
at which movements for human liberation are struggling to
be born. Following Cone's biblical emphasis upon God's rev-
elation *within* historical events, our task is to examine the
spirits at work among us in order to know if any may be of
God.

If God is active within the white community, where might
we look for his hand at work? Once the issue is raised in this
fashion, many cultural movements come to mind, with the
central one being a complex of protests, values, and life-
styles usually referred to as the "counterculture" composed of
the children of the white middle class. It should be clear at
the beginning, however, that in pointing to the counterculture as evidence of the divine initiative for our liberation,
no attempt is made to ignore the inconsistencies and the
demonic influences which pervade the youth culture. Before
the Exodus was over, many of the Hebrew children were
cursing Moses and worshiping pagan deities, but the event
was the agency of redemption nonetheless. In some such
fashion it can be said that ideas, values, and aspirations
being spun off by the young hold great promise for our liberation.

It is not necessary to impugn the integrity of those who
fought in Indo-China to argue that the refusal of so many
young men to obey the command of their government to go
to war has been among the most important contributions of
youth today. By the very fact of their continued exile in

domestic prisons and in foreign countries they are bearing witness that there are human values which transcend the claims of the state, and in doing so they force the question which is basic to the captivity of Protestantism. When Billy Graham preached before the Lincoln Memorial on July 4, some Mennonite youths raised a banner which read, "Hour of Decision: God or Country?" The white churches have to face that question before their own exodus can begin. I see in the raising of that question itself, the hand of God opening a way for white Protestantism to escape its bondage to the cultural status quo.

In spite of all the bizarre and dangerous implications of the fascination of the young with occult practices and their willingness to experiment with drugs, their manifest hunger for religious experience is a telling indictment of the churches. The hungry sheep, having waited at the feet of shepherds who were unwilling or unable to feed them, finally got together and left the fold.

While theologians and preachers fret about the meaninglessness of religious language, the children of middle-class white Protestants are so starved for spiritual nourishment that they have gone out to fill their emptiness with whatever is available, from hardcore fundamentalism to Zen Buddhism; from every bizarre occult practice to the earth mysticism of the American Indians; from Science of Mind to hallucinogenic drug trips. In this connection it remains to be seen what effect, if any, the Jesus movement will have on the churches now that its day in the journalistic sun appears to have ended. There are signs that the main thrust of the movement was easily diverted into politically safe channels by the clever entrepreneurs who work the fringes of evangelical Protestantism. But there are also intimations of a new social concern among the theologically conservative branches of white Protestantism. Regardless of what many may think, the divorce between social activism and evangelical fervor is a recent, and probably temporary, phenomenon. If the two should come together again, the major shifts in national priorities which are remote possibilities now would become realistic opportunities.

In any case, the Jesus movement must be kept in proper perspective as but one of the many evidences of spiritual renewal. The importance of Eastern forms of spirituality and the renewal of Indian tribal religions should not be underestimated. A related and perhaps more powerful aspect of contemporary youth culture is the quest for what are thought to be natural, truly human relationships with one another and with the earth. The romantic illusion in this is obvious, but here again there is something very exciting going on.

In its extreme forms the new quest for "natural" relationships leads to an outright rejection of technology, yet a moment's serious reflection on the human situation would indicate that such a position is neither possible nor moral. Nevertheless, it calls into question the complicity of the churches in the rise of a technocratic society in which the production of frivolous abundance has run wild, with the consequent destruction of nature and impoverishment of the human spirit. A Wintu Indian has asked, "How can the earth like the white man? . . . Everywhere the white man has touched it, it is sore." American Protestantism, growing up as one motivating force behind a people's conquest of a wilderness, has tended to view such notions as hopelessly sentimental.

Is it merely sentimental to worry about the lengths to which the despoilation of the planet may go? The energy crisis has brought home to us the reality of the finite character of the earth's resources. No doubt we shall eventually harness the sun, the sea, and the atom in such a way as to release their power to us in a safe and efficient manner. But the question of our relationship to the created order is spiritual and ethical as well as physical. It is this dimension of the ecological crisis, recognized early on in the counter-culture, which may be seen as an opening for religious renewal.

It is commonplace to say that we are in a period of unprecedented technological innovation. But we have been very slow in facing up to the social consequences of this fact. Rapid technological advance brings with it social changes which are very frequently detrimental to human welfare, and while people grow more and more dissatisfied with the pace and quality of their lives, they do not generally recognize the source of the problem. We have the technical means to achieve almost any material goal, but there is neither rhyme nor reason to what we do. Operating with the sole value of unrestrained growth, our technological proficiency spins out super-kill weapons and no-return bottles in equally mindless profusion. Ironically, those who suffer the greatest disillusionment at the present time are those who are presumably in the best position to inherit the first fruits of abundance: middle-class white Americans.

It would be very easy to overplay the theme of the white people as an "oppressed" group, but the discontent which gnaws at the vitals of middle America at the present time cannot be ignored. *New York Times* editor James Reston noted a few years ago that what we were gaining on the surface in the form of a higher standard of living was being offset by a sense of loss in our hearts, a declining sense that our lives are in tune with our best moral instincts. Unprecedented affluence has created "the new poor," whose deprivation is not material, but social, psychological, and spiritual.

In a peculiar and hardly definable way, many members of the white Protestant community feel that they, too, are under siege at the present moment in our national life. They, too, feel oppressed and exploited, with the added frustration that they are not sure just whom they should blame for their plight. It would be hard to trace all the dimensions of this feeling. There have been constant angry confrontations over race, poverty, and the war. The cities are overcrowded; the air and water are polluted; the purity of food is suspect. Inflation soars; traffic congestion intensifies; crime rates mount. Work becomes increasingly humdrum, and the contrived stimuli to consume more and more subvert the joys of ownership. One cannot afford to be sick or expect to send his children to the better schools.

Many of these things affect us all, of course, but the disillusionment is particularly bitter for those who have presumably met all the preconditions laid down in tradition for entry into the abundant life. Think of those who through thick and thin have stood up for "what is right with America." This silent majority finally got their team in the White House under the banner of a return to decency, law, and order. Imagine the dismay of the silent believers when *their* administration turned out to be the most corrupt in American history. Is there nothing sacred anymore? Where will it all end?

The spiritual impoverishment of white existence has been dramatized by the effect of black studies courses on the white students who have attended them. The WASP student encounters there an ethnic richness which he has never known, and he realizes that "his own upbringing and education have joined together to rob him of any specific cultural awareness." [3] In the present emotional malaise, we are beginning to realize that white people have become disconnected from their own traditions, and that the renewal of the best in our particular cultural heritage is a matter of urgent concern.

There is enough truth in all this to substantiate the claim that the "oppressor" is himself increasingly victimized by forces over which he has, as yet, no effective controls. The basic symptom of the white man's dehumanization by these forces is a sense of spiritual loss—which returns us once more to the failure of white Protestantism° to provide a strong moral presence at the point of social policy-making on the one hand, and a resource for the meaningful nurture of souls on the other. There is the dark cloud's silver lining: perhaps the crisis will bring a new openness to the possibility of discerning God's presence at those points in our situation where movements of human liberation are taking shape.

It is as though every crisis is an opportunity to recapture the vision of God's presence in human affairs, for all the movements related to the loss of the human center of life are important for theological reflection. All these dynamics could be illustrated by reference to the women's liberation movement alone. As women break away from their own peculiar bondage in a male dominated world, the judgments they raise against men become the occasion for new insight and growth for men as well as women. In the light of all that is happening in our generation, can some basic affirmations of faith be recovered in a way which will have particular relevance to white Protestant Americans?

VII.
Another King
Than Caesar

Many contemporary theologians feel that the central theological problem of our time resides in the fact that religious language is used, but not understood in the churches. While this observation undoubtedly contains a measure of truth, it is a mistake to assume that language itself is the problem. Religious language is vital only when it points to a reality which is present in the experience of those who use it. If the sense of personal encounter with the ultimate is gone, no amount of semantic shuffling will bring it back.

The most fundamental question for theology must always be the reality of God. This is not to refer so much to the debate over God's "existence," as to the understanding of the reality—if any—toward which the use of such a symbol as g-o-d might be meaningfully employed. Such is really to ask if the relation of man to the universe is ultimately characterized by neutrality, hostility, or benevolence. Granting that many would deny the necessity of the question itself, some such choice is implicit in the way we live our lives. Since that is the case, a personal decision at this primitive level of awareness is decisive in determining the religious bent of one's life.

That the universe was called into being by a sovereign deity and operates according to his will is a key assumption of the American religious heritage, even in its most distorted forms. Among Protestants, this affirmation—in somewhat different guises—was made by both New England Puritanism and the Enlightenment Anglicanism of the founding fathers of the nation. In both movements, the belief was solidly buttressed by human reason: a kind of biblical scholasticism on the one hand, and an appeal to natural law on the other.

Whatever their many faults, the English Puritans who established the Massachusetts Bay Colony saw an intrinsic incompatibility between the sovereignty of God and political tyranny. For all our pious and patriotic protestations to the contrary, this fundamental affirmation of our forefathers has actually been reversed in mainline American religion. As we have indicated earlier, belief in God and subservience to whatever the political process produces are thought to be synonymous. Is it any wonder that faith in the God proclaimed by the established churches is increasingly problematical? I am convinced that there is within our own ethnic heritage a theological tradition so explosive in its promise that America will never be the same again if it is recovered.

The sixth chapter of Isaiah begins with the words, "In the year that King Uzziah died I saw the Lord sitting upon a throne." There is no time like the faltering of principalities and powers to recover the reality of the kingly rule of God. The political crisis of America in the wake of the Watergate scandal constitutes a theological opportunity which must not be missed. It is a ripe moment for the smashing of idols and therefore a propitious time for extending human freedom, for the source of all bondage is idolatry.

Idolatry and Easy Belief

Arthur Miller's play, "The Death of a Salesman," is the story of the disintegration of a man's life. The chief character in the play, Willy Loman, had decided as a young man that the key to happiness, the way to give meaning to life in this world, is making a lot of money. He was inspired by his successful brother Ben, who described his financial ventures by saying, "When I walked into the jungle, I was seventeen. When I walked out I was twenty-one. And, by God, I was rich!" [1] Concluding that the best way to make a lot of money was to become a great salesman, Willy Loman spent his life under the delusion that he was indeed on the verge of a great financial breakthrough, and that he was building an empire as he drove countless miles over his New England territory.

As the play opens, however, Willy Loman is 63 years old, and he is not even making enough money to pay the premiums on his life insurance. The people he had counted on to give him his big break were either retired or dead. His sons, now in their thirties, have no respect for him and have not followed his advice concerning the importance of financial success. The older boy can't keep a job more than a month. The other's chief interest is in making out with women.

The play ends with Willy Loman's utter defeat and ultimate suicide. Standing beside his father's grave, Loman's older son says, "He never knew who he was. . . . The man didn't know who he was." [2] Willy Loman never knew who he was because he sought his identity in the wrong place, because he trusted a vain hope to validate ultimately his life. On one level his life might be seen as a Puritan life-style which has been drained of its vital essence, a lively sense of the reality of God's presence in the world. In this regard his life is typically middle American: the frenetic pursuit of the ever-transient dream that someday all the disparate elements of our hoping will come together in fulfillment.

The circumstances of human life are so structured as to make the matter of choosing a god to worship and serve almost unavoidable. In his catechism Martin Luther asks,

"What is it to have a god?" In the answer to that question he says, "That to which your heart clings and entrusts itself is, I say, really your God." [3] Each one of us has many concerns, many loves, many things we hope for and work toward. This is, of course, as it should be. But it is crucially important to establish priorities, to know what concerns us ultimately. One of the most important insights of the Old Testament is its abhorrence of idolatry. To give first place in our lives to any earthly goal or power is to court eventual disillusionment.

In one way or another I have repeatedly referred to the reality of political idolatry in America. In Nazi Germany when most of the people, including most of the Christians, were swept away on a tide of pagan worship of the Fuehrer and the Fatherland, a small number of Christians formed the Confessing Church to resist Hitler. Their rallying cry was, *Der Herr ist Gott!* "The Lord is God!" Before such a slogan could serve the purposes of human liberation in America, a far more subtle form of idolatry would have to be faced, an idolatry which permeates popular religion itself.

The inability of all the time, energy, and money put into religious activity to satisfy the spiritual hunger of contemporary America is related to our tendency to trivialize whatever is holy. Almost every new stirring of the sacred is met by the mentality of the entrepreneur: How can we insure the *success* of this new movement of the Spirit? By *selling* it, of course! Thus it happens that the name of Jesus is most often seen and heard today in the context of slogans and jingles. We wear Jesus T-shirts, insert his name in soft drink commercials, hip-hooray him like a football hero, and attempt to promote a marketable image for the crucified rabbi of Galilee. We can hardly recommend Jesus more highly than by pointing out that he has been favorably mentioned by some astronaut, quarterback, or beauty queen. And I saw the sovereign Lord of the Universe positively likened to a popular mouthwash in a church bulletin: "God is like Scope; he always refreshes."

Implicit in this whole approach to religion is the assumption that faith in God can be quite an asset to you in doing your thing, whether that be the search for the perfect surf or making a fortune in the stock market. Jesus will heal your pimples and make your personality pleasant. He is closer to you than the golden arches of the nearest Mac-Donald's and just as predictable. Give him a try! Is this the only doctrine of God white Protestants can offer to a nation which inwardly starves for some dimension of experience which is holy and incorruptible?

If God is valued because he is *useful* to us this must necessarily mean that he is subservient to some other value in our lives, and therefore not truly God. For as long as we inquire into how and in what ways God may be useful to us, for so long the experience of worship will wither and die. Worship which is truly worship addresses what God is in and of himself, although just what this might mean is now and probably ever shall be a deep and impenetrable mystery. Is there a Roman Catholic church in the country which is not packed to the walls for the midnight Mass on Christmas eve? Among those who gather on that holy night are increasing numbers of Protestant young people, hoping to come for a brief moment into the unmistakable presence of ineffable mystery.

There is a clear relationship between the sense of spiritual loss and the prevalence of idolatry. We have taken a lot of mileage from political idolatry, but recent events have so tarnished the images involved that this brand of Americanity is faltering. Popular Protestantism still knows how to turn a current fad into a boost for religious enterprises, but for many there is an aching emptiness within which cannot be filled any longer by the cotton candy of superficial piety. For myself, it has been a long struggle, but I think that I have begun to put into place the basic building blocks of a personal faith which attempts to come to terms with the biblical witness without denying the realities of life in the twentieth century.

Must We Be Safe to Be Saved?

My first year in seminary was—in a spiritual sense—the darkest year of my life. The warm glow which seemed to light my path after the initial decision to enter the ministry had long since faded. My college career had bequeathed to me many unanswered questions which were about to drive me not only from the ministry, but out of the Christian community altogether.

In the beginning, at least, seminary was only adding insult to the injury. I was so despondent that after reading Luther's comments on the impossibility of saving oneself by human effort, I wrote that he was surely correct and added that he was fortunate to be expressing such sentiments from the perspective of faith. Personally, I had no faith and Luther seemed only to confirm a growing suspicion that I never would.

I was not really a cynic, either, for I remember how I used to identify with that beautiful passage, "As the hart panteth after the water brooks, so panteth my soul after thee, O God" (Ps. 42:1 KJV). It was simply that on the rational level I could no longer give credence to the basic doctrines of the faith as I understood them. The warm encounters with Christ which others reported from their prayer groups simply never happened to me.

My despair as a student began to lift as I persisted in reading the Reformers and their contemporary interpreters. It began to dawn upon me that my despair was related to the fact that the faith options which I had been aware of were pale shadows of the full import of the biblical witness. Most of the people I knew understood faith either as the ability to believe the church's teachings or as an encounter with certain feeling experiences which were understood to be confirmations of Christ's presence. Most people seemed to emphasize both.

Understand that I had not really questioned these assumptions; I had simply been unable either to believe or feel in the prescribed ways. Now I was beginning to see that our relation to God may not be determined either by what we believe or how we feel. The notion that God accepts or loves people because they hold what he considers to be proper opinions and experience feelings which he either initiates or approves seemed to me blatantly contrary to the spirit of the New Testament. Since my own basic hang-up was a rational one, Martin Luther's comment on Psalm five hit me right between the eyes: "It is by living, by dying, by being damned that one becomes a theologian, not by understanding, reading, and speculating!" [4]

I began to realize that some of us find meaning in life in the same way we become theologians. We begin with life, our own personal existence, and not with dogma or theory of any sort. Thinking is a way of clarifying, understanding, and articulating human experience and, as such, it is essential to becoming a mature person. But my gloom began to dissipate when I recognized that there are no *absolutely* verifiable answers—in either reason or experience—to some of life's most basic questions, and that, furthermore, such verification is not prerequisite to meaningful life anyway.

Viktor Frankl wrote that "a man should not ask what the meaning of life is. . . . He must recognize that it is *he* who is asked." [5] I learned that faith is not so much finding the answers to my questions, as it is facing up to the one big question: my own personal existence. At last, at a very primitive level, I began to answer that question. In the deepest recesses of my soul, I knew the experience described by Dag Hammarskjöld: "At some moment I did answer *yes* to Someone—or Something—and from that hour I was certain that existence is meaningful." [6]

Does this mean that I decided to believe in "the existence of God"? No! It means that I decided to *trust* God and, for me at least, trusting God came to mean affirming life, saying *yes* to my own personal existence. I had no part in the creation of the universe, no control over my own birth, and no responsibility for the shape history was in when I first saw the light of day. The world was simply given, and I was part of it for good or ill. Faith at the most primitive level is saying *yes* to this basic situation.

It is important to say this, because it still seems to me that faith for many is a way of turning aside from the world, of escaping some of the fundamental realities in their lives. The gospel is "good news" for some because it seems to grant a certain immunity to the vicissitudes of history and human experience, particularly to the reality of death. But I believe that faith in the incarnate Lord is synonymous with a total immersion of myself into what is human, an affirmation of earthly existence in full awareness of the anxiety inherent in personal relationships on the one hand and the threat of physical suffering and death on the other.

Some would no doubt find it difficult to understand how I can say that the theologian who helped me most in recovering a vital faith was Rudolf Bultmann and that the contemporary book which meant most was his *Jesus Christ and Mythology*. Listen: "To believe in the Word of God means to abandon all merely human security and thus to overcome the despair which arises from the attempt to find security, an attempt which is always vain. . . . Faith is the abandonment of man's own security and the readiness to find security only in the unseen beyond, in God." [7]

The radical import of this understanding of faith really becomes clear when under the category of "merely human security" is included the whole ecclesiastical framework and along with it all the religious movements and theological systems ever devised, including Bultmann's. This is what the unfortunate phrase "religionless Christianity" was all about: radical confidence in God undermines all human presumptions of whatever sort.

It would be a mistake, however, to assume that the notion of "security in the unseen beyond" reintroduces an escape hatch in the face of the tragedy of history, a way of getting along in the world without taking the human dilemma seriously. On the contrary, it is precisely this sort of "freedom from the world" that enables the man of faith to be free *for* the world, to live in it, and love it.

Out of his experience in a Nazi concentration camp, Bonhoeffer wrote, "Only those who weep for the Jews may sing Gregorian chants." He was saying that faith is truly vital only to those who are fully conscious of the tragic character of history and human experience.

What all of this means to me may be summed up in an offhand remark I once heard Carlyle Marney make: "You don't have to be *safe* to be saved." No, the priest still lives under the same threats to his life as the atheist, and the judge may die before the thief. The point is that one comes to faith by being radically open to life as it is.

When the question is raised as to whether there is *any* frame of reference in which the creation can be understood to be meaningful and just, I think I am strongly influenced by the Calvinists. I believe that God knows what he is doing whether I understand it or not. Who really knows? In a cosmic perspective, to be sure, we are a very minute aspect of what is going on in the universe, and in the limitless span of eternity, the life of Earth is but a moment. Faith assumes that the universal process is somehow benevolent, that for the Creator to take the chance that what *has* happened would happen, is somehow just. The ultimate meaning of creation is known only to God, and that is all right with me.

We do not have to have all the answers to be able to live with joy and meaning, but we ought at least to be sure we are not evading the crucial questions. The affirmation of personal existence, the celebrating of the life which has been given, is by no means all there is to be said about faith—but it is the place to begin.

Allen Ginsberg and Jonathan Edwards

As the two hundredth anniversary of the nation's birth draws near, we might attempt to recover something of the original impulse of our Puritan forebears at the point of their distinctive emphasis upon the sovereignty of God. This doctrine is the politically revolutionary notion which is at the heart of the Protestant heritage: to be radically bound to God is to be radically free from all forms of tyranny. But when we move from autobiographical reflection to the broad arena of history, the concept of the sovereignty of God, as usually understood, is very difficult to maintain. That God is both supremely powerful and completely benevolent is surely not self-evident today, and we are unable—in the face of the atrocities we have known—to say with impassive Puritan resolve that contemporary world history is unfolding under the watchful eye of a sovereign deity who cares.

How, given the evils we must acknowledge in our own history, can we speak of God? As a boy, I rejected once and for all the sorry notion that all the evil and misery in human history exist for the purpose of determining who will spend eternity having a pleasant time in heaven and who will ever-lastingly languish in the flames of hell. Even with all my adolescent hang-ups I could already announce to my parents that I considered myself morally superior to any such God and that I was prepared to demonstrate that superiority by declining to enter the pearly gates should they ever open in my direction.

All the years since have only further convinced me that there is an inverse relationship between belief in the God who presides over heaven and hell and genuine moral concern. Ten years in campus ministry likewise indicate that the more convinced a student is that he is personally destined to wake up in heaven, the less interested that student is going to be in attempting to do something about what is happening in this present age. The more concern for souls, the less concern for bodies. That begins to look like a law to me.

So, what now? In Archibald MacLeish's famous play *J.B.*, the haunting refrain continually recurs:

> If God is God He is not good,
> If God is good He is not God.[8]

In the final analysis, our picture of God must be focused through the lens of what we know of Jesus Christ, and what we know of him is anything but the cool detachment which is implied by omnipotence. I personally find it impossible to believe that God is all-powerful, all-knowing, and all-loving —and, if forced to omit any one of the three, it would have to be the first. The explanation which is sometimes given— that while God is all-powerful, he is presently working under the constraints of self-imposed limitations—only makes matters worse. That is the ultimate expression of bad faith: refusing to do what you are able to do, on the ground that your *role* in a situation forbids it.

Under the extraordinary circumstances of the Nazi holocaust, Dietrich Bonhoeffer wrote from his prison cell, "Only a suffering God can help." There may be those who would argue that such a view is not only inconsistent with Protestant theology, but also heretical. I do not think that this is the case. Who in the Christian community would challenge the assertion that "God is love"? Daniel Day Williams has written that "If being and love are inseparable, then being and suffering are inseparable. . . . If God does not suffer, then his love is separated from the profoundest human experiences of love, and the suffering of Jesus is unintelligible as the communication of God's love to man." [9] If the gospel of Jesus Christ means anything, it means that God is not only *for* us, but *with* us as well.

How can we appeal for a new appreciation of the sovereignty of God and say at the same time that the lessons of history negate his omnipotence? The answer to the dilemma is to be found in the Puritan tradition itself, in the thought of Jonathan Edwards. It is unfortunate in the extreme that this greatest of American theologians is represented to American students almost entirely by his infamous sermon, "Sinners in the Hands of an Angry God." (This is as good an example as any that is likely to come to mind of the distortion of the WASP religious heritage.) For Edwards, God's sovereignty was an expression of absolute love rather than absolute power; not a legal concept, but an "aesthetic experience." In certain situations there comes to one the *sense* of God's presence in the world, and that apprehension is of a mysterious reality at the heart of nature and history which can only be described as "beautiful."

Protestantism in America tends to draw a line between those who think and those who feel, between the rationalists and the revivalists. The same tendency can be seen in the immensely popular "sensitivity" groups in which an anti-intellectual bias is encountered in the often repeated admonition, "get out of your head." What is needed is a rediscovery of the possibility of thoughtful feeling, or sensory thinking. This may, in fact, be the most promising opening on the contemporary scene for a new apprehension of the sovereign love of God. If it does not stagger the imagination too much, I would like to draw what I feel to be a striking comparison between the poet Allen Ginsberg and Jonathan Edwards as a way of showing how close we are in the contemporary spiritual quest to rekindling a distinctly white Protestant emphasis upon the sovereignty of God.

In a poem entitled "Transcription of Organ Music," Ginsberg describes how, while sitting in a room listening to recorded organ music, the room seemed to be closing in on him. For relief, he walked outdoors into a backyard flower garden. There in the night he saw flowers with their heads poised, uplifted, waiting for the return of the sun. In that moment all creation seemed to him to be opened to the sky, waiting to receive. He felt that *he* was, too. Later he wrote, "I had a moment of clarity, saw the feeling in the heart of things, walked out into the garden, crying." The poem concludes:

> I want people to bow as they see me and say
>   he is gifted with poetry, he has seen
>   the presence of the Creator.
> And the Creator gave me a shot of his presence
>   to gratify my wish, so as not to cheat
>   me of my yearning for him.[10]

This almost ecstatic glimpse of "the feeling in the heart of things," which is occasioned largely by the consciousness of the mystery which surrounds and pervades the individual person and reaches to the outer limits of the universe, is not comparable to the earthy sentimentality which is so character-istic of many in the back-to-nature movement. Ginsberg's thoughts plunge immediately into social reality: "The world knows the love that's in its breast as in the flower, the suffer-ing lonely world. The Father is merciful."

In a similar fashion, Jonathan Edwards rejoiced in the sense of God's presence in the created order. He would walk alone in the woods and pastures and even find a sheltered spot which would give him a good view of the lightning during a storm. In his journal he wrote of a particular day. "As I was walking . . . and looking up on the sky and clouds, there came into my mind so sweet a sense of the glorious majesty and grace of God. . . . The appearance of every-thing was altered. . . . God's excellency, his wisdom, his puri-ty and love, seemed to appear in everything; in the sun, moon, and stars; in the clouds and blue sky; in the grass, flowers and trees; in the water, and all nature." [11] On such occasions, Edwards says that he would sing aloud of his joy-ful awareness of the "Creator and Redeemer." Christians who want to be as tough as the demands of obedience require at the present time without losing a personal sense of inner freedom and joy may find in Jonathan Edwards a helpful model.

There is no necessity for white Protestant youth to go begging for blessings from someone else's religious heritage if they are willing to exert the effort required to rediscover our own. To experience the richness of all human stories is important and not to be devalued, but that is a process which requires giving as well as taking. We can appreciate another story best when we have learned to tell our own.

I believe that Allen Ginsberg, although he may belong chronologically to an earlier generation, symbolizes several dimensions of the counterculture which come together to open new possibilities for faith. He combines a sense of moral outrage at the actions of government with a sensitivity to the mystery which he calls "the feeling in the heart of things." Those of us who, as a group, seem most responsible for waging war and spoiling the environment have within our own religious heritage a theological resource for responding to this situation. As a start, we have begun to reflect upon the doctrine of the sovereignty of God, and to recover from Jonathan Edwards the possibility of sensory thinking as a means toward a new apprehension of the reign of God's love.

When there is no lively sense of the presence of God in our lives we are subject to all sorts of idolatry and tyranny. Those who are not guided by what the heart knows as the holy Presence transcending all being will eventually bow their knees to some very worldly power. For all their own tendencies toward absolutism, our Puritan fathers knew this one thing: only God is the Lord. The sovereignty of God does not mean that he controls or even allows whatever is happening. It means that in the midst of whatever is happening, I will submit to no claim, bow my head to no authority, salute no flag, which does not make allowance for the prior claim of God upon my life. I see no other way to be truly free.

Praise God Anyhow

I have been unable to reason my way to a faith in God that is vital to my everyday experience of life in the world. Furthermore, I have come to the conclusion that it is futile to make the attempt. As I will indicate later on, I have no particular complaint to lodge with those who profess to be atheists on the grounds that belief in God is irrational, given the evidence available to support that belief. Even if it

were possible to demonstrate the existence of God with flaw-
less logic such proof would be of little value.

The story is told of the philosophy professor who asked a
class of sophomores how many of them were convinced that
God exists. No hands were raised. He then outlined all the
classical proofs for the existence of God and called for someone to refute the arguments. None was able to do so. "Now,"
he asked, "how many of you believe that God exists?" No
hands were raised. I think of this story whenever I am "witnessed" to by someone who has been trained by the Campus
Crusade for Christ. Their pattern is to begin getting affirmative responses to fairly simple questions which must
necessarily lead you to recognize that God not only exists,
but is logically bound to obey four "spiritual laws." All such
approaches fail to see that if the existence of God could be
shown to be rationally necessary, *faith* would not only be
unnecessary, but impossible.

The response of faith is evoked by the sense we have of
the *beyond* which may come to us under such widely varying
circumstances as joy, sorrow, beauty, wonder, and many
others. In his classic work, *The Tragic Sense of Life,* the
Spanish philosopher Unamuno says that "it is not rational
necessity but vital anguish that impels us to believe
in God." [12] Peter Berger, an American sociologist, has recently argued that the human capacity for joyful play is likewise
a "signal of transcendence." It is in both the heights and
depths of human experience that we encounter the ineffable,
mysterious source of all being. When the death-of-God debate of the sixties was at the peak of its intensity, claiming
the cover story in *Time* magazine and catapulting Thomas
Altizer and a few others into the limelight of public attention, I found a striking theological affirmation in an unlike-
ly place. In front of a drug store on a sign usually reserved
for promoting patent medicine specials were three words,

Praise God Anyhow. That the store was in Birmingham, and owned and operated by black people, added more power to the impact of this timely admonition. There was no attempt to argue the case, no effort to answer the charges raised, nothing to suggest the trivializing God-is-alive-I-talked-to-him-this-morning response of the bumper stickers. Praise God anyhow, and get on with the business of living and dying, weeping and laughing, dancing and mourning, working and playing. It is good advice.

VIII.
How Original
Is Sin?

Armed robberies were not all that unusual in Detroit: over 13,000 had been reported in the year before. But this one was different. The young black man behind the gun this time had recently been called to the White House where President Lyndon B. Johnson had placed around his neck the Congressional Medal of Honor. Going for his own gun beneath the counter, the grocer had no way of finding out who Dwight Johnson was before he answered the demand for money with a hail of bullets.

There is no way of telling the whole story. But one day in Vietnam, after seeing his closest friends blown up in a nearby tank, Johnson had retaliated in a reckless rage, single-handedly searching out and killing from five to twenty of the attackers. He came home and joined the ranks of many other jobless vets, until the day came months later which brought the call from Washington. There followed months of lavish attention from just about everybody—banquet after banquet, fancy car courtesy of a major motor company. The Army lured him back as the finest conceivable recruiter of young blacks for the service.

What was going on in the tortured soul of the young man nobody could fully appreciate. There were the horrors he had seen face to face, then the sudden celebrity status for his actions in the midst of those horrors. In all the thousands of pats to the back and pumpings of the hand, did anybody know or even care? Then there were the mounting debts, the growing depression, and, finally, the fateful episode in the corner store, apparently undertaken to raise the money needed to get his wife out of the hospital where she had gone for minor surgery. Had he lived another week, Dwight Johnson would have been twenty-four years old.[1]

Who is there to blame for such a tragedy? The grocer? The Army? The Viet Cong? The president? All of us? What could I have done about it, or you? What is it in the human situation that brings us ever and again to the shedding of our brothers' blood? Do we all stand so strongly under the legacy of Cain that we are doomed to go on killing each other forever?

The story of Dwight Johnson is doubly tragic and ironical when, in the context of our whole discussion in this book, it is recalled that a similar episode occurred after World War II, involving a red man rather than a black. One of the most memorable scenes from that war was captured in a photograph by Joe Rosenthal. He snapped for the Associated Press the dramatic picture of six battle-weary Marines as they hoisted the American flag on Mt. Suribachi following a hard fought victory at Iwo Jima. A monument based upon the photograph was created and placed as a memorial in Arlington National Cemetery. Only three of the six men in the picture lived to see the end of the war. One was Ira Hayes, an Indian of the Pima tribe.

The New York *Times* reported on January 25, 1955, that Hayes had died at the age of thirty-two, when he apparently passed out after some heavy drinking and remained exposed to a severe winter night on a reservation in the Arizona desert. Reviewing a television play based on his life, a critic wrote: "Hayes was bitter over the treatment of Pima Indians. . . . His drinking was increased because of his awareness that he did not agree he was heroic for the reasons generally assumed. Similarly, he could not abide the dubious patriotism that prompted some of the ceremonies in his honor." [2] In life Ira Hayes frequently served as a symbol of all the things Americans like to remember about themselves; in death he became, as did Dwight Johnson after him, a symbol of that side of our national reality which all of us too easily forget. It is a dimension of social reality which might be illumined by the old concept of sin.

The Dangers of Innocence

In his State of the Union address to Congress and the American people in early 1974, President Nixon introduced an appeal which is usually all but irresistible to us: an invitation to forget the past in order to concentrate on the future. "One year of Watergate is enough," he said, and senators and representatives anxious about the loss of public confidence in politicians responded with vigorous applause. Let us not *dwell on the past*. Let us not call attention to what is *wrong* with America, but to what is *right* with America!

This is appealing rhetoric until it is viewed in a different light. Can you imagine yourself at the conclusion of a physical examination, insisting upon a report which emphasizes your excellent eyesight and plays down the significance of that dark shadow the X ray detected in your lungs? We have a very strong tendency to do precisely this when it comes to an assessment of our health as a nation. President Nixon is not the first national leader who, when lethal toxins have been discovered in the political bloodstream, has gone about the country saying, "I have seen the heart of America and the heart of America is good."

After the race riots wrecked the national image of Birmingham, we launched a massive campaign to reconvince our-

selves that we were O.K. Billboards, newspapers, television—
all urged us to say something good about Birmingham, liter-
ally to be sure that we spoke favorably to each other about
the city every day. Emphasize the fact that our churches are
numerous and beautiful, not that guards are posted at the
doors to prevent black folks from entering to pray! But what
pulled our city out of its nose dive was not slogans, but
the social surgery of those who had the courage to read the
real diagnosis of the trouble.

If we ever knew it at all, have we already forgotten that in
1972 our Christmas assault on Hanoi and Haiphong was
"the heaviest conventional bombing campaign in the history
of mankind"? This Advent slaughter of the innocents—that
is, the many civilians who perished—was justified as the
only way we were able to get the concessions needed to
bring the peace negotiations to fruition. One year later jour-
nalist Anthony Lewis pointed out that, as a matter of fact,
the terms of peace were not significantly influenced by that
massive display of violence. And, Lewis wrote, it is important
to bring the matter up now, *lest we forget.*[3]

America needs a mature understanding of what the Christian doctrine of sin is all about. But a tenacious clinging to
the notion of our fundamental innocence is one of the most
dominant characteristics of our national temperament. This
persistent sense of innocence is itself the chief manifestation
of the reality about which the ancient doctrine of original
sin speaks. In the classical Greek tragedies the most fundamental fault of humanity is identified as pride (*hubris*),
the inclination which is in every one of us toward an exag-
gerated sense of our own virtues and accomplishments. Although the concept has been variously interpreted and vigorously denounced by those of a liberal and optimistic temperament, the Christian view is essentially the same: it is

universally the case that undue self-regard leads to the corruption of all human enterprises.

In *The Quiet American,* Graham Greene writes that "innocence is like a dumb leper who has lost his bell, wandering the world, meaning no harm." Properly understood, the Christian doctrine of original sin would lead us to the realization that we must guard ourselves as much against all simplistic reassertions of the mood of innocence as against the pathological obsession with guilt. Some popular movements of late, such as the Jesus movement, the back-to-nature movement and others, have attempted to short-circuit this issue and rejuvenate the classic American assumption of innocence. We stand in need of a massive infusion of realism in our doctrine of man, and I think the heritage of the Reformation can help us find it.

Lewis Mumford, one of the most persistent analysts of where history is taking the human family, has argued that people who are motivated by a sense of blamelessness are "a greater block to the renewal of life today than the most brutal dictators, whose nefarious designs often awaken the very opposition and struggle that produce change." While this is a rather extravagant claim, Mumford's point is crucial to that rekindling of conscience which we sorely need. In a passage explicitly dealing with the importance of the concept of sin, he writes, "The passionate murderer may repent: the disloyal friend may regret his faithlessness and fulfill his obligations of friendship: but the average man, who has obeyed the rules and meticulously filled out all the legal papers, may glory in what he is—and that is a deeper misfortune; for it is in his name, and by his connivance, precisely because he sees no need for changing his mind or rectifying his ways, that our society slips from misfortune to crisis and from crisis to catastrophe." [4] Surely one of our greatest problems today is the deficiency and narrowness of our sense of sin.

The Weightier Matters of the Law

In his angry tirade against the Pharisees Jesus says, "Woe to you, scribes and Pharisees, hypocrites! for you tithe mint and dill and cummin, and have neglected the weightier matters of the law, justice and mercy and faith; these you ought to have done, without neglecting the others" (Matt. 23:23). It is one of the ironies of the white Protestant experience in America that we who, in popular opinion, are responsible for laying such a heavy load of guilt upon people must now be called to account for abandoning our own heritage at the point of its emphasis upon the scope and scale of the problem of sin.

In recent years popular Protestantism has fallen into the trap of those who, in Jesus' words, "strain out gnats and swallow camels." But it is important to know that there are theological reasons for this development, that our restricted understanding of sin is the result of a narrow perception of what is vital in religion. In his study of southern white Protestantism, Samuel S. Hill has shown how the frontier experience, rural life-style, and cultural isolation created and preserved a version of Christianity which has as its basic preoccupation the salvation of the individual soul, made manifest in the experience of conversion, and expressed through the quest for personal purity.[5] His analysis rings true to my own experience.

Whenever we understand faith to be a highly individual and intimately personal affair, our concept of sin will be cast within moralistic contours. If we understand the requirements of Christian obedience in terms of keeping oneself *pure,* our ethical concerns will tend to be prohibitive in character: a Christian is one who does *not* do certain things. A Christian does not speak profanely, does not drink alcoholic beverages, does not violate the Lord's day, does not steal, gamble, or lust after the things of the flesh.

Images from adolescence in Alabama flood my mind. In high school I was sent before the Honor Council for gambling because I matched coins with several other boys in order to determine who would carry the trays back when we had finished lunch in the school cafeteria. Pointing out that casting lots was a biblical way of deciding things did not strengthen my case before a jury of my peers, and I was placed on probationary status. One of my friends told his mother that if she would let him go to the movies on Sunday just this one time, he would promise not to enjoy it. She got the point and let him go. Most of all, we did our part to prepare the way for Hugh Hefner's fame and fortune by making sex such a taboo subject that we thought the word "immoral" necessarily had something to do with sex. Without arguing against the validity of our concerns in any of these areas, I am saying that many of us have been trained in an understanding of right and wrong which leaves us unable to comprehend the weightier matters of the law. And I have come to find out that this experience is by no means limited to the South.

The minor problem with a moralistic assessment of the problem of sin is that it tends to foster the kinds of behavior it seeks to prohibit. In Sunday school once, our teacher was giving the college class its monthly lesson on temperance. "Surveys show that 74 percent of students drink beverage alcohol at some time during their college years," she said. From the back of the room, a voice replied, "We're a hundred percent at Sewanee!" Turning around in a corporate state of shock, we learned that the audacious utterance had been issued from the throat of the son of one of our church's leading laymen. He went on to confess that he first began to think about sampling a beer out of the curiosity aroused by our pastor's frequent references to the evil. Willie Morris makes the case well when, describing his childhood experience in a church in Yazoo City, Mississippi, he writes, "It is an axiom of human nature that if you hear how easy and sinful something is, and if you hear it long enough and frequently enough, and you are warned not to think about it, your thoughts will head that way just of their own volition." [6] That is the minor problem with moralism: it really does not work.

The chief problem with moralism from a Christian point of view is that it is untrue to the spirit of the New Testament. Although history has been far too hard on the Pharisees, it is nevertheless true that they are presented in the gospels as being precisely the kind of people Jesus was *not*. In the interest of human welfare, Jesus violated the sabbath, refused to condemn prostitutes, consorted with sinners, and was accused of being a winebibber and glutton who would not teach his disciples the virtue of fasting. He did not see this behavior as a true violation of the Law, but as a fulfillment of the Law in its essence. This attitude is seen most clearly in his saying, "The sabbath was made for man, not man for the sabbath" (Mark 2:27).

One of the most traumatic moments in my life came when, as a young minister, I heard the governing board of a large Methodist church decide—without a dissenting vote—to turn black people away from the door, should any appear at the hour appointed for worship. The situation is impossible to understand unless it is realized that most of the people involved genuinely could not see the relationship between segregation and religion. The important thing was for everybody—black, white or otherwise—to get their hearts right with God and live according to the mores of the community.

In pursuit of these ends anybody was free to start his own church if he so desired. To create any kind of disturbance where an intimate relationship with God was being formally fostered was unthinkable. There was no theological basis in the religion as it was being practiced which could have contributed to the formation of Christian social doctrine.

Again we should say that this situation, while clearly seen in the South of the sixties, is in no way limited to that region. Much that we have said in previous pages argued the case for Christian complicity in the preservation of political policies which have meant suffering and death for multitudes. It is of the utmost importance now that white Protestants realize that this failure to perceive the true character of the human situation and the consequent insensitivity to the grossest of sins is a relatively recent *distortion* of their true heritage.

The thought of Roger Williams' spiritual offspring settled into an easy alliance with official bigotry is difficult to entertain. He was exiled from Massachusetts for his opposition to government policies, specifically those policies which exploited the Indians. And those who think of themselves as evangelical Christians would do well to study the example of the Methodist circuit riders who did as much as anybody else in the early days of America to spread democratic social ideals. Francis Asbury, the first of the galloping preachers of the frontier and the first bishop of American Methodism wrote, "We must suffer *with* if we labor *for* the poor." His advice was taken to heart by those who followed him: "Year after year they found shelter in dirty cabins, slept in comfortless beds, and shared the meager fare of the poorest of the poor." [7] Before we can begin to recover this heritage of compassionate concern, we must learn to recognize the manifold forms which evil takes in modern America.

Stone Walls a Prison Make,
and Iron Bars a Cage

In early September, 1971, America was jolted by the news that forty-two persons had been killed when 1,000 state troopers, sheriff's deputies and prison guards stormed the Attica Correctional Facility in New York to end a rebellion taking place within the walls. Striking inmates had held some thirty-eight hostages in an encampment in the prison yard for four days. The bloodbath which ended the episode was, with the exception of the Indian massacres in the late nineteenth century, "the bloodiest one-day encounter between Americans since the Civil War." Exactly two years later, I asked a class of some thirty college students if the word "Attica" reminded them of anything specific, and only two were able to recall the event.

The New Testament specifically enjoins the Christian community to "remember those in prison as if you were there with them" (Heb. 13:3). We do not take the words seriously for two basic reasons. Most of us assume that fundamental American institutions are virtually sacred and that the authority of those who run them ought to be respected. And in the case of prisons, we assume that those who are there are getting what they deserve. This latter assumption is itself a reflection of our understanding of sin in very narrow terms: the willful violation of a prohibition by an individual. There is no more direct way to heighten our consciousness of the corporate and institutional character of sin than to remember those who are in prison.

Since so many have lately done so, there is no need to recount in these pages all the horrors of the American system of jails and prisons. It should be enough to say that, for the most part, they constitute a grossly inhuman environment of violence and cruelty. The buildings are typically very old, fortress-like structures. At least five hundred were built in the nineteenth century. Inside, human beings are kept in cages, and many cells could not pass the space and sanitation codes required for the confinement of apes at the zoo. When the late Swiss theologian, Karl Barth, toured an American prison, he said that the experience had been "like walking through Dante's vision of hell."

These days it is generally assumed, even by many professionals in the corrections field, that prisons do not rehabilitate and that most of those who leave will come back. Prisons do indeed perform an educational function; they are so effective in reinforcing antisocial attitudes that they have been called "universities of crime." It is crucial to remember that the tuition, some 1.5 billion dollars annually, is paid by people like you and me. The more significant costs, the human consequences of *both* crime and punishment, are incalculable.

In terms of our discussion, the critical point concerns those among us who feel the impact of the criminal justice system most keenly. The answer to that question is, "Prisoners today are poor, and they are black. Arrested more often, held without bail more frequently, less likely to have their cases dismissed by the prosecutor, frequently forced to hire third-rate attorneys, they are found guilty more often sentenced more often to prisons for longer terms, and more often denied parole." [8] Although black people comprise a small minority of the United States population, they constitute as much as one-half the prison population in some states (such as California) .

That inmates in correctional institutions come in large degree from the poorer members of our society can be shown in several ways. Perhaps the most shocking indication of this reality is the fact that a substantial proportion of those who are in jail at this moment have not been *convicted* of the offense for which they are being held. Approximately one-half of those in city and county jails are there because they cannot afford to pay bail. This means that many—because of the great backlog of cases waiting to be tried in the large urban centers—will spend as much as eighteen months in jail while they are presumed to be innocent under our system of justice.[9]

Although we picture Justice as a lady wearing a blindfold and evenly measuring right and wrong for all sorts and conditions of men, the fact is that the likelihood of being jailed for a criminal act, no matter how serious, varies in direct proportion to the financial resources of the person committing the offense. This inequity in the operation of the law was dramatically underscored by a landmark decision of the California State Supreme Court. Two men had been found guilty of jointly committing a crime and were fined $3,000 each. One of the men was able to pay the fine and went free; the other could not pay and was, therefore, sentenced to spend three hundred days in jail. On appeal, the court ruled that the second man had been denied his constitutional right to equal protection under the 14th amendment and ordered him released on probation.[10]

This court decision is notable because it breaks with a time-honored precedent. However, since the operation of our system of criminal justice continues to favor the prosperous, we can say that those who are in jails and prisons are for the most part the economically disadvantaged who are either waiting for trials or serving sentences. There being a high correlation between skin pigmentation and economic status—the darker the skin, the lower the income—the higher proportion of "colorful" persons incarcerated is a built-in feature of our social system.

During the week that these words were written the newspapers reported that Lieutenant William L. Calley had been set free under a bail bond of one thousand dollars pending appeal of his case. Do you recall his crime? He was convicted of murdering twenty-two Vietnamese civilians in the village of My Lai, surely one of the most notorious crimes by an individual in our nation's history. In the white glare of national interest and concern, a military court sentenced him to life imprisonment at hard labor. As a matter of fact, he has merely been confined to his apartment at Fort Benning, Georgia, and he is now free. The stated reason for his release was the judge's assumption that he might already have served too long a sentence, given the certain review of his case and almost inevitable further reduction of the sentence.

It is impossible not to compare this decision to the misery of the thousands who, never knowing the advantages of meaningful education or decent food and housing, now waste their lives away in modern dungeons for the desperate writing of bad checks and for stealing stereos. One must think also of the meager punishments meted out to those who by their own admission have conspired to subvert the essential political mechanisms by means of which the nation itself survives. They were engaged in no less a crime than the violation of all the individual freedoms won in the American Revolution. Ask yourself how the system has dealt with them and compare it to the fate of a George Jackson who was serving his eleventh year for a seventy-dollar robbery when he was killed in San Quentin. Put it all up against the fate of a law-and-order vice-president who—in the same year that he pled guilty to one crime upon the promise that he would not be indicted for others and resigned in disgrace—was himself given around-the-clock protection at government expense and earning an income in six figures.

Again, who is there to blame?—not so much for the crimes, but for the grossly inequitable response they evoke from us as a people, expressed through the systems we have devised.

It is in this corporate sense that we must recover the implications of the doctrine of original sin. The overriding sin of white people in America today is our own prideful assumption of innocence. If neither you nor I have personally robbed and killed, we must nevertheless come to the point of assuming responsibility for the consequences of those social processes which depend upon our implied consent for their continued operation. Further, our conscious sense of blamelessness suppresses an unconscious guilt whose destructive influence is the very core of racism. This truth is nowhere better seen than in the way our judicial system separates the sheep from the goats.

The Sense of Sin and the Capacity to Hope

In one of his novels Albert Camus tells the story of a lawyer who understood himself to be a very good man. There was concrete evidence to point to, such as his willingness to defend clients others would shun and the frequency with which he took the cases of those unable to pay for his services. Everything was fine until a personal experience brought home to him the realization of what he called "the fundamental duplicity of the human being." He had learned, he said, that "modesty helped me to shine, humility to conquer, and virtue to oppress." [11] It is a fundamental teaching of orthodox Christianity that all men and women are sinners, and most notably so when they begin to flaunt their innocence.

Commenting upon the fall of Spiro Agnew, columnist Gary Wills writes:

The odd thing is that those who so "theologize" our patriotism neglect the very theology that feeds the images. . . . A conviction of sinlessness is the ultimate sin. Those who feel they have to flatter their country are, in the last analysis, flattering themselves. And that is the very definition of vice—or the pride that leads to the fall—in the theological world on whose rhetoric Agnew depended. The saints of Western Christendom were those who arrived, sincerely, at the basic truth—that they were sinners. . . . They were simply stating, in their own eyes, the obvious—that the way to get in touch with reality is to know how flawed and broken every man, every human thing, is.[12]

To insist upon the discussion of sin is not to draw a dark veil over the joys of human existence, but rather to introduce a consciousness of reality without which our very humanity is not safe. It has been the thesis of this chapter that the basic spiritual fault of America is a proud sense of innocence which blinds us to our very real crimes against the human family including, of course, ourselves. In the context of this whole book, we are saying that the most heinous of these crimes are catalogued in the continuing chronicle of the white majority's dealing with the more colorful peoples both at home and abroad. Now we have said that the sinners' call to repentance must come from within their own heritage, from the Christian doctrine of original sin. We must add that, properly understood, this doctrine is not just a cultural feature to be neutrally acknowledged or, more often, negatively judged.

It comes as no surprise to any who have followed his previous concerns that America's best-known psychiatrist should write a book dealing with the urgency of our recovering a sense of sin. It is Karl Menninger's long and compassionate concern for human welfare, perhaps most notably his prophetic judgment upon our system of criminal justice, which led him to write *Whatever Became of Sin?* He argues that our troubles today result in part from our having a lively sense of neurotics to be treated and criminals to be punished, but almost no sense of sinners who need repentance and forgiveness. Recalling our previous discussion of what has happened to our sense of the holy, we might also say that the concept of sin has been trivialized. Our capacity for moral indignation is so blunted that we can live in the midst of the most outrageous events imaginable and be unable to feel any sense of personal responsibility. We have found it possible to watch the evening news on television and enjoy dinner at the same time.

But Menninger's purpose in writing is not to increase our depression and despair. "Sin is the only hopeful view," he says, because it is only a renewed sense of personal responsibility and accountability which can return a sense of hope to our world.[13] But prosperous white Americans in particular, those who are closest to the seats of power, have a hard time thinking of themselves as sinners in anything more than the trivial sense of eating and drinking too much on occasion. We are "nice" people and our friends are nice people.

But, as Menninger reminds us, if we are all basically nice people, how do we account for the inconceivable atrocities which have been carried out in your name and mine? We have to say that nice people somehow get together in the perpetuation of designs which have disastrous consequences for their fellow human beings. Nice people owned slaves, conspired to destroy the native American peoples, and dropped the napalm on Vietnamese villages, and all acted with the consent of the multitudes of nice people who cast the votes and surrendered the dollars in taxes. None could watch the Watergate proceedings without being struck by how "nice" and respectable were the persons in the parade of witnesses. It is by pointing beyond specific "sins" to the basic dilemma of our humanness that the doctrine of original sin illumines the social and corporate dimensions of evil.

Reinhold Niebuhr was one of the few American theologians in this century who saw and attempted to apply the abiding truths inherent in those traditional doctrines of Christianity which were the touchstones of the Protestant Reformation. Concerning original sin, he wrote:

> Collective pride is . . . man's last, and in some respects most pathetic, effort to deny the determinate and contingent character of his existence: The very essence of human sin is in it. This form of human sin is also most fruitful of human guilt, that is, of objective, social and historical evil.

> Prophetic religion had its very inception in a conflict with national self-deification. Beginning with Amos, all the great Hebrew prophets challenged the simple identification between God and the nation, or the naive confidence of the nation in its exclusive relation to God.[14]

This is the challenge which is before us now. Let it be clear that this is not a call for striking pious poses in sackcloth and ashes as though, once more, our problem goes no deeper than public relations.

In calling for a renewal of the concept and awareness of sin, Menninger uses an image which is very helpful. If you were one of a dozen people in a lifeboat and discovered a leak near the place where you were sitting, would there be any doubt in your mind concerning your responsibility? Whether you actually *made* the puncture or not, to ignore it would be the functional equivalent of having made it. I believe that the whole American experiment is in danger of sinking and that white Protestants are in a position very near the hole. If we can bring ourselves to acknowledge its presence immediately, there is still time to act.

IX.
God Shed His Grace

Utilizing the psychological techniques devised by Ira Progoff, I recently found it possible to get back to some of my early childhood experiences and gain new insights into myself and into the dynamics of Christian faith. At a workshop I attended, it was explained that Progoff's method involved techniques of writing in a personal "intensive journal" which would lead to progressively deeper insights. We were asked to divide our lives into definable periods, then attempt to remember in writing some important episodes from one of these periods. Although I was somewhat skeptical about the whole process, I decided to see what memories I could bring to consciousness from my preschool years.

These were years when I spent a lot of time alone with my mother while my father worked and my brother and sister were in school. The scene which came back to me most vividly was washday. My mother would gather all the soiled clothes and linens and pile them on the kitchen floor beside an old wringer-type washing machine. As the washing proceeded, I tumbled about in this little mountain of towels, sheets, shirts, and such. As I wrote, strong sense perceptions returned. Lying on my back in those clothes I would watch a steaming white tongue of wet linens squeezing through the wringers and arching downward in my direction on the floor. Once again I could hear the sound of the released water splashing back into the tub and sense the sweet, pure smell of the steam rising from the tight, heavy mound of clean clothes building in the basket beside me on the floor.

I recalled that sometimes, as we were nearing the end of one of these washday wonderlands, we would hear footsteps on the stairs leading up to the backyard porch, and my mother would ask, "Who is *that?*" I knew it would be my father arriving home after an extended night shift on his job at a factory—which would have been making cotton gins had the outbreak of war in the Pacific not caused it to begin making rocket casings at a feverish pace. As the door opened and my father picked me up to kissing height, I would ask in a small, hopeful voice, "What did you *bring* me?" And he would answer with a question, "Have you been a good boy today?" At this point we would both look in my mother's direction for the answer. She never gave anything less than a qualified affirmative in those early days, and my father would open his lunch box and bring out chewing gum, peanuts, or candy purchased from a machine at the plant.

I was writing for the first time in the intensive journal, and this seemed to be the end of the installment. But after a moment I began to ask myself why I remembered this particular set of circumstances and not some other. Then, as though it were from some deep, hidden valley in my brain, an anonymous voice asked, "Have you been a good boy today?" Then I began to imagine the question asked in unison by a great chorus of people: schoolteachers, preachers, aunts and uncles, policemen and judges, merchants and lawyers, friends and total strangers.

And suddenly I knew with unmistakable clarity what I had dimly sensed for years: that my whole existence as a person bears the dominant impress of that question. The family, the church, the school, and the whole of Southern culture as I knew it were obsessed with the question of personal goodness—one might even say *cleanliness* to round out the metaphor. "Have you been a good boy?" I would go so far as to say that my initial decision to enter the ministry, made at the age of sixteen, was at the psychological level an attempt to answer that question once and for all.

So what? The point for me in all this is that the retelling of my personal story in this way not only brought new insight into the dynamics of my own behavior, but also opened in renewed freshness the deeper dimensions of that story we have come to call the gospel. It is this latter story which eventually led me to see, not only that in a world like this the only honest answer to the question of personal innocence must always be *no,* but also that this negative need not be utterly debilitating. It is precisely this realization which is needed by white Protestant Americans if we are ever to move beyond the present cultural impasse. We must rediscover that graciousness at the heart of things which rises up to meet us in the depths of personal confrontation with ourselves, that gracious word which says that who you have been need no longer tyrannize over who you *are,* and who you might become.

The Bad News and the Good News

The film, *Easy Rider,* in which three young men ride motorcycles across the country on a kind of vain search for the soul of America, has been compared to a prophetic saying of Amos. He spoke of a famine "not of bread, nor of thirst for water," but a famine of hearing the words of the Lord. He said that young men and women would wander from sea to sea seeking the word of the Lord without finding it (see Amos 8:11-13). That is precisely what has happened to thousands of young white Protestants in this generation. Spiritually, they are listening, but they hear the churches bringing down "bad news."

Jesus compared the kingdom of God to a treasure hidden in a field, which a servant found and in great joy sold everything he had in order to buy the field and possess the treasure. Our use of this parable in sermons shows how far we have strayed from our biblical moorings. We have often used it in support of our *demands:* "if you would enter the kingdom of God, first do this and that." But the great New Testament scholar Joachim Jeremias has called our attention to the fact that the emphasis of the parable is upon the joyful surprise, an unexpected and undeserved discovery which motivates the servant to respond as he did.

Jesus did not come saying—as so many of his spokesmen do—"you *should,* you *ought,* you *must* . . . ." His gospel is seen as much in what he did as in what he said: kneeling beside the adultress, going home with Zacchaeus, drinking from the Samaritan's cup, taking the children in his arms, blessing blind Bartimaeus. Even the Ten Commandments, always visualized as inflexibly graven in stone, are preceded by the announcement of a real event, to which the keeping of the law is a response: "I am the Lord your God, who brought you out of the land . . . of bondage" (Exod. 20:2). "I *am* the Lord your God," not "I *will be* the Lord your God if . . ." In like manner, Jesus' gospel is not primarily an idea, not a law, not a principle to be understood. It is an event, an engagement in which we are met by Another who is gracious to us, who does not in the first instance put pressure upon us to do right or espouse proper opinions. When the good news happens, we know that we are who we *are* and that we are *accepted.* The struggle to be thought well of by others subsides as the divine *yes* surges through our being.

It is only at this moment that profound personal change can occur, the sort of change that flows from within rather than responding to external threats and pressures. The chief barrier to such change is pride, the will toward self-justification which we discussed in the previous chapter as the essence of original sin. Since the hallmark of the Reformation faith was "grace alone," we can see the irony of white Protestant America bolstering the national facade of prideful innocence: America is great because she is good. But enough has been said concerning our dilemma. How do we get at the good news, specifically the good news as it relates to white Protestant Americans?

The Word Made Skin

Eugene O'Neill's *The Iceman Cometh* is a play which is set in the backroom of a rundown bar in a depressed section of New York City. The characters include a washed-out revolutionary who spends most of his time in a stupor, and Harry Hope, the owner, who has not been outside the place in years, but constantly talks about going out, getting to know the people, and being elected alderman. There is a prostitute who frequents the place, always talking of her plans to get married and settle down on a farm. She will marry another character in the bar, who, although he has been unemployed for a long time, expects to find a job soon.

These characters and a few others spend their days sitting around in the bar, drinking and dreaming of what they are going to do in the future. Their wretched lives are perked up twice a year by the visits of a traveling salesman named Hickey who buys drinks for all and tells a lot of jokes. When Hickey arrives this time, however, he has experienced a severe trauma in his own life which leads him to feel that he must force all to face the fact that their intentions are merely pipe dreams which will never come true. In this way he robs all the characters of their illusions, with the result that all sink into despair, grow to hate each other, and become embroiled in violence and death.

On one level, as the title suggests, this play might be understood as a reversal of Christian faith. Most people must somehow intoxicate themselves, either by drink or illusions, in order to guard against the awareness of what life is really like. The Christian longing for the return of Christ is perhaps the grandest illusion of all, for if the *truth* should be revealed in its stark reality, things would get a lot worse rather than a lot better. It is my opinion that, instead of brushing this play aside as the fruit of one man's bitterness, we would do well to have it read and discussed in the churches.

First of all, we should respond to this play with the confession that, on the everyday level of our lives, it is a word of judgment against us. It is a characteristically American thing to assume that *someday* our lives are going to be really happy. We are a future-oriented society. When we graduate, when we get that new car or boat and get a better job, when the children get a little older, when we build that place in the mountains or by the lake, when we save enough to go to Europe or Hawaii, when we retire—*then* we will be truly happy and fulfilled. *Then* we will "have it made." The expectation of a life of joy and meaning *later,* having a future goal which gives to every "now" the character of preparation or prelude, is typically American.

In the second place, we should be aware of how this attitude, when translated into religious terms, causes us to emphasize one dimension of Christian belief to such an extent as to obscure the very core of the faith. Many have turned their Christian experience into a waiting game: if we are only good enough, if we only believe fervently enough, pray hard enough, give generously enough, *someday* Christ will come and take us home to receive our just reward. This present world is but a testing ground, only a place we are passing through on our way somewhere else.

While there is an element of truth in this future orientation, it is by no means representative of the gospel in its fullness. For the gospel to *be* the gospel it cannot be spoken in the future tense. The gospel is good news, not because of what it promises, but because of what it proclaims: *God is with us.* That is a word which must be spoken in the present tense. Nothing is clearer in Jesus' preaching than the proclamation of the present reality of the reign of God's love. Let us frankly acknowledge that this is a difficult notion to grasp and that most of us act as though we do not believe it. But it is this doctrine, the doctrine of the Incarnation, which is the key to theological renewal in our time and place.

To think seriously about the gospel of the Incarnation is to encounter once more the same problem we have in connection with our doctrine of God: we can only conceive of the divine presence in terms of *power*. Since this is admittedly a very rotten world, how can we imagine God's presence *in* it? If he were truly in it, could things be the way they are? No, it is better to believe that Christ is the one who is yet to come than to say that he has come and makes so little difference. In reality the Incarnation as we understand it is something like this: "The Word was made flesh and dwelt among us. Then the Word left, but we hope that someday the Word will return with enough power to straighten things out." Billy Graham refers to Christ's return in power "with the armies of Heaven." As if it were not bad enough to imagine that there are armies in heaven, we have also to assume that, in some very important sense, God is not *with us* after all.

When Paul prayed to be delivered from some unidentified physical impairment, he received this answer to his prayer, "My grace is sufficient for you, for my power is made perfect in weakness" (II Cor. 12:9). It is in some such way that we must come to understand the Incarnation, the mode of God's presence in the contemporary world. As Father Avery Dulles has recently written: "Incarnation does not provide us with a ladder by which to escape from the ambiguities of life and scale the heights of heaven. Rather, it enables us to burrow deep into the heart of planet Earth and find it shimmering with divinity." [1] The good news from Bethlehem so long ago is still good news for America today. We will discover God's gracious presence among us only when we know where to look, and toward the clouds of heaven is not the place to fix our gaze.

In his first public utterance Jesus is said to have read from the book of Isaiah, "The Spirit of the Lord is upon me,/because he has anointed me to preach good news to the poor" (Luke 4:18). We all know that "Christ" means "anointed," but we fail to connect this anointing with good news to the poor. This connection, however, is unmistakably clear in the New Testament. The followers of John specifically asked Jesus if he were the Christ and he answered, "Go and tell John what you have seen and heard: . . . the poor have good news preached to them" (Luke 7:22). It should not surprise us in the least that the contemporary manifestation of the Incarnation is occurring among the colorful peoples of the world, in the Third World. The key to locating the incarnate word is given in the statement, "He is who he was."

An Affirmation of Whiteness

At this point in the discussion it is, perhaps, past the time to bring forward several strands of the argument to see if they do not converge in such fashion as to make visible a new manifestation of Christ the Redeemer, graciously opening a new and surprising path toward the future. If, as

James Cone insists of Christ, that "he is who he was," we can expect to find a dialectic at work in his contemporary appearance. For when he came into Jerusalem, he both provoked violence and inspired nonviolence. His condemnation of the temple was a sign of its renewal; his dying brought a new surge of life to many.

Protestantism has reached its present state of affluence by means of its accommodation to native sentiments about the American destiny. By belonging to Caesar in this way, white Protestantism has never fully belonged to Christ; it has never been able to work at transforming its culture in terms of the reconciling work of the Spirit. Indeed, by sharing the assumption of the melting-pot image of America, the churches have been active—if unwitting—agents of dehumanization, best illustrated by our mission to the Indians.

For a complex variety of reasons, the power of American nativism to hold the society together is greatly diminished, most notably so in the militant ethnic consciousness of colorful Americans and the disaffection of white young people. Being in a virtually Christless condition, white Protestantism is bedridden by the same fever which is sapping the vitality of Caesar. At the same time there has come bold and energetic leadership from the ranks of the black churches. That leadership and the revolutionary impetus it has spun off among blacks outside the church structures is being interpreted as the contemporary self-disclosure of God.

God is present among us by means of his identification with the black liberation struggle and with similar movements against oppression and exploitation. Christ is present in America today, and Christ is "black." It follows that Christ is calling into judgment all white-dominated national institutions, the churches not least of all. In theological perspective, it must be said that the pervasive sense of guilt which is dogging the heels of the powerful in this country is the work of the black Christ. The crucial question for white Protestants is how we are going to deal with this crisis. It is a very uncomfortable position we occupy, one analogous to that of the Pharisees and Sadducees. We, who presume to be defenders of the faith, face an unavoidable indictment drawn up precisely in terms of that faith.

But if, indeed, Christ is who he was, it is fair to ask if he still weeps for Jerusalem. Does he seek the *total* destruction of this admittedly oppressive society? Perhaps it *is* true that "not one stone will be left standing," but is this a suitable *goal* for theological thinking? In a previous discussion we suggested that all the spirits seeking the liberation of the oppressed may not be of God. We cited the analysis of Harold Cruse to the effect that in a society so far advanced as ours technologically, true revolutionary change must be understood in terms of a revolution in consciousness. Specifically, what is needed is a new awareness of the ethnically pluralistic character of the society. It is not to abandon the struggle for liberation to argue that change must flow from this realization if it is to be truly worthwhile and lasting.

We went on to say that the realization of ethnic pluralism requires the emergence of a new white consciousness and that a theology which addresses itself to white reality could facilitate such a process. We are now ready to speak of the other side of the dialectic brought into play by the manifestation of Christ in blackness. Although he is reluctant to speak about it, Cone acknowledges that one result of the liberation of oppressed peoples is the liberation of those who oppress them. This sentiment was always present in the expressed aspirations of the late Martin Luther King, Jr. At the conclusion of successful demonstrations in Birmingham, he expressed gratitude to God in these terms: "He has clearly been at work among us. And it is He alone who has finally gained the victory for ALL his children."

The sooner white people recognize in the present crisis the seeds of our own liberation, the better it will be for us all. Christ's *no!* to the old order of white domination reverberates in a profound *yes!* to a new realization of white humanity. In spite of all their faults, many young white people are moving out to say *yes* to a life which does not need to dominate others or ravage the earth in order to validate itself. In them Christ is calling us to affirm our own existence as human beings who happen to be clothed in white skin. He is freeing us from the demonic strains of our past and thereby making it possible for us to mine the rich seams of our own buried heritage for the purpose of bringing out precious gifts to offer for the enrichment of all mankind.

As long as we hear the gospel telling us that we are chained to the oppressive sins of our forefathers and cannot be free until every drop of retribution has been wrung from us as heirs to their perfidy, our only hope is to justify ourselves by attempting to defend the past—or to explain away the inequities of the present on the ground that there is no humanly realizable better future, as so many evangelicals do. In either case, the gospel is *bad* news which does not set anyone free within the setting of contemporary historical realities.

But to hear that the power of white domination is already broken and that anyone among us is free to walk through the rubble of that broken wall and into the arms of Christ his brother is to discover a priceless treasure. And that is the *good* news which is beginning to make itself heard through the chaos of the present. The resounding *yes* to one's ethnic reality is the contemporary realization of the wider reaches of the gospel. The joyful cry, "Black is beautiful!" echoes in "I'd rather be Red!" and "Yellow is mellow!" By harmonizing with these refrains, rather than shouting them down, one may also express gratitude to Jesus Christ in saying, "White is all right."

X.
Toward Liberty
and Justice

The familiar story in the first book of Samuel about David's encounter with the Philistine giant, Goliath, has both humorous and informative aspects. Once David had convinced the army officers that he should be allowed to do battle with the giant, King Saul removed his own royal armor and placed it upon the courageous young man: a bronze helmet, a coat of mail, and a mighty sword. It must have been a very dramatic gesture. But then, the scripture says, David "tried in vain to go." With all that heavy equipment, he could not even walk, much less fight a giant! So he decided to take it all off and go to the stream to look for some good slingshot stones.

As an older generation welcomes the young into the arenas of business, politics, education, and all the rest, it inevitably says, "Here are the structures within which we operate. *Put them on.*" But we have survived as long as we have, kept the monsters away from the door as long as we have, only because there have been some in every generation who have said to one King Saul after another, "These structures are too heavy for me. I have to go at things in a simpler, more direct fashion. I'm willing to take some big risks in order to see if I can make a difference in the way the struggle is going." This is the process of renewal, the dynamic of social change and progress, and these considerations are of crucial importance at the present moment in our national life.

Our particular concern is with the implications of Christian obedience for white Protestant Americans today. An army of Goliaths is ranged against us in the form of forces which have been set in motion by our own history. In the situation that faces us, what is Christian obedience? How can we find the resources to do what is required of us? The problem as we have analyzed it is that the answer to the first question has been framed too cheaply in terms of the requirements of Caesar, and the answer to the second with an implied or overt appeal to his power. When discipleship and citizenship are equated in this fashion, the element of social transcendence is lost; society stagnates, and the church loses touch with its own soul.

We have spoken of the sovereignty of God and of the liberating influence of his gracious actions in Jesus Christ. Perhaps we should now point to the biblical evidences of the presence of the Holy Spirit. The book of Acts begins with the dramatic assertion, "You shall receive power when the Holy Spirit has come upon you" (Acts 1:8), and the story moves ahead from there to demonstrate what such empowerment means. It was the presence of the Spirit among them which enabled the apostles to confront judges and kings with the confession, "We must obey God rather than men." How far that is from the chorus which echoed in Jesus' ears as he climbed his last, lonely hill: "We have no king but Caesar!"

Harden our hearts against it as we will, we must not deny that in our own generation we have witnessed a resurgence of the kind of courage which goes before the seats of power to say, "We must obey God rather than men." Obviously, not everyone who disobeys Caesar does so in order to obey God! But in the Civil Rights movement and in the opposition to

the war in Indo-China it once again became commonplace
to find persons going to jail for the sake of what they felt to
be a higher claim upon their obedience than the civil government's. Such phenomena may be interpreted in Christian
terms as the Spirit present to teach us once more that the
essence of being human is obedience to the sovereign Lord of
creation. When final obedience is reserved exclusively for
God, one is truly free from earthly bondage.

This is the Reformation understanding of man as completely free and completely bound. By being bound in obedience to God, one is released from the shackles of worldly tyrants even though they imprison him. The problem is that
we human beings have a strong inclination to consider the
freedom of others as a threat to our own, as though freedom
is a natural resource which is being rapidly depleted. In order to secure our own prerogatives we resort again and again
to the enslavement, in one way or another, of our brothers
and sisters. It is the continuing work of the Spirit to liberate
not only the enslaved brother and sister, but also to free the
slavemaster from his own misguided perception of what it
takes to insure his own well-being.

The implications of the Spirit's contemporary manifestation are many for the white Protestant community, and we
shall not be able to do more than suggest the mood and direction of our liberation in the economic, political, and social
realms. We must take as a presupposition the fact which
Protestants are prone to ignore, namely, that the questions
of personal meaning and social responsibility are inextricab-
ly intertwined. I am convinced beyond the shadow of a
doubt that it is possible to go through an entire life doing
the things that respectability requires and saying the things
you are expected to say, that is, to live a "blameless" life,
only to wake up some morning and realize that it has all
been devoid of any real depth of meaning. The sooner one

begins to ask questions about the character of the institutional frames of reference which set the conditions of life for us
and for the many, the better it is for all concerned. To ask
such questions in the light of the biblical witness is the essence of the Protestant heritage.

Beyond Works Righteousness

One of the significant contributions of the Reformation
was the expansion of the concept of "a calling" to include the
most humble occupation as no less an opportunity to serve
God than the priesthood. In the evolution of this idea
through Puritanism and the development of the so-called free
enterprise economy, it has come to be transformed into something rather different from what Luther himself might have
envisioned. Rather than cobblers mending shoes as an expression of gratitude for the grace of God, Americans have
come to seek their own self-justification through the agency
of work. White-hot ambition which drives a person to sacrifice everything, including his own health, in the pursuit of
status, security, money, power, and honor is generally recognized as a virtue.

The social implications of this contribution of white Protestantism to America are many. While the consciousness
which was shaped by this understanding was a great stimulus
to the conquering of the frontier and the rapid economic
development of the country, its continuance has long since
passed the point of diminishing returns. For one thing, the
productive apparatus it created is out of control, threatening the destruction of the environment in many ways. In
terms of linking human needs with the supply of goods and
services, the system seems to be breaking down. The nature
of work itself and the rationale for doing it have increasingly
become dehumanizing for those who are within the system.

The religious character of work makes it extraordinarily difficult to think of alternatives and requires that the poor be treated as heretics.

Those who have encountered the good news of human liberation in Jesus Christ are in the best position to say, "I am who I am, not what I do." The notion that a person's worth must be measured in terms of the job he or she does is blatantly contrary to the original Protestant emphasis upon the primacy of God's grace, not to mention the Pauline discussion of faith over works. In an age of automated abundance it becomes less and less possible—or necessary—to provide jobs for all who need them. And among those who do have jobs, perhaps not even a majority will be performing tasks which they find meaningful. In this situation, the religious reinforcement of the prevailing conviction that everyone must not only have a job, but also find meaning in it, is personally cruel and socially regressive.

We might begin to consider that one's "work" and one's "job" need not necessarily coincide. I know young people with college degrees who wash dishes, drive cabs, sack groceries, and such because, since their avocation is the theater, music, art, and poetry, there are few jobs available which would allow them to earn a living by doing what they feel called to do. In fact our system of linking survival, not to mention respectability, to the job exerts enormous pressures which militate against the flowering of creativity and genius. The banality of American culture, which reaches its absolute nadir in television, is the logical result of a system which values the creativity of its writers and film-makers only to the extent to which their talents can be successfully utilized in marketing mouthwash.

Without glossing over the ambiguities in the position of those who drop out of the system, the recent unwillingness of some white youths to justify their existence in terms of a career might be used for the sake of us all by the Spirit who works for human liberation. In our acquiescence to the task-masters of the world we have too often placed a bargain price on our souls, on our own sense of personal worth and self-esteem. But we should bear in mind that merely letting some-one else run the system—old or young, black or white, man or woman—will not produce revolutionary change. That kind of change will follow only when we cease attempting to justify ourselves through the medium of the mad race to acquire.

It is right and proper for those outside the system to step up their demands for a share in its benefits. At the same time, if change is to come, there must be those inside the system who turn their backs upon the lures of career and affluence. It is only in this way that the values which inform the present order can be undermined, and a new consciousness developed which will bring in its wake a changed system. We are wager-ing that the system can be subverted to a revolutionary de-gree whenever enough people realize that material ambition is ultimately vain, and that the attempt to justify one's ex-istence through worldly success is finally empty.

Revolution for the Sake of Order

Throughout this book every indictment of church and na-tion has been balanced by an affirmation of the evidence for hope. By disengaging itself from its parasitical relation-ship to the dying illusion that America has been appointed God's guardian of the world, white Protestantism will be liberated to discover his presence in the midst of contempo-rary events. A real encounter with the divine will lead to the promotion of a theological integrity which cannot fail to reconnect us with the authentic Protestant heritage and thereby give us a new sense of common identity. The Indian intellectual, Vine Deloria, Jr., says of us that unless we "achieve a sense of historical participation as a people," we cannot survive. To the great good fortune of both the church and the nation, our roots are in that strain of the Protestant heritage which is revolutionary in character.

It is the Reformation emphasis upon the sovereignty of God, rather than the Enlightenment notion of the dignity of man, which is the real revolutionary power to transform American culture. While the latter dies the death of a thousand reasonable compromises in political expression, the former's appeal to transcendent reality always returns to judge the powerful. It was the Puritan's belief in the sovereignty of God that led him to say *no*! to tyranny and find himself thereby embroiled in political controversy. As Michael Walzer has shown, the English Puritans in the late sixteenth and early seventeenth centuries found their obedience to God forcing them into political roles. Some fled into exile where the necessity of structuring community life would not allow the political questions to recede. Those who remained in or returned to England became revolutionaries.

Walzer's thesis is that the English Puritans were the originators of radical politics. The techniques of free assembly, mass petition, group pressure, and appeal to public opinion all grew out of the efforts of Protestant clergymen.[1] The point is that the white Protestant theological heritage is at home in a revolutionary situation. It should be noticed, however, that the Puritan activists were motivated by a desire to achieve the kind of social stability they could live with theologically and ethically. It may be the case that our revolutionary heritage can be rekindled through the realization of those who long for "law and order" that stability will never come without dramatic and far-reaching social change.

The reason stability requires revolutionary change in

our situation is that the current chaos stems precisely from the nature of the present "order." Philip Slater argues that it is the emerging technocratic society which breeds contempt for age and tradition, worships novelty, systematically invalidates knowledge and experience, and turns its back upon community and family ties.[2] Even a successful president of a large corporation has written that the leaders of all our major institutions operate on the basis of wrong assumptions and has called for "dismantling our organizations where we're serving them, leaving only the parts where they're serving us." It is crucially important for us to realize that it is the present "order" which is destroying us as a nation and as a church.

Finally, as we have said all along, we must be sure that our revolution is revolutionary. William Stringfellow contrasts Barabbas and Jesus as revolutionaries and provides valuable insight. The first model is that of the insurrectionist whose obsession is with the seizure of power and who is therefore easily dealt with by tyrants because he has the same character as they. The second revolutionary style is far more dangerous to oppressors, because Jesus' revolution is "empirical": he has experienced, come to terms with, the pervasive power of sin and death in the world and transcended it. The mature Christian is a free man already in the sense that he is no longer intimidated by the forces of death.[3] Not depending upon any agency of this world for the consciousness of his own worth, he is a dangerous man indeed.

In the lives of black men such as Martin Luther King, Jr., we have seen the revolutionary power of this latter consciousness at work. We see it at work in whole ethnic communities getting themselves together. The time has come for a generation of persons who are no less free and no less Christian because they are white. Our own history calls out to us in the words of an address to the English Parliament by the Reverend Thomas Case in 1641: "Reformation must be universal. . . . Reform all places, all persons and callings; reform the benches of judgment . . . reform the universities, reform the cities, reform the countries, reform inferior schools of learning, reform the Sabbath, reform the ordinances, the worship of God. . . . You have more work to do than I can speak. . . . Every plant which my heavenly father hath not planted must be rooted up." [4] It sounds impossible, the noisy rhetoric of preachers. But listen: a black man has been the sheriff of a county in south Alabama for more than eight years now. Fifteen years ago he would have faced difficulty attempting to vote. As we have said all along, putting a black man in an office does not usher in the kingdom of God, but believe me, when a black person becomes the chief law enforcement officer in Macon County, there has been a radical transfer of power. The system is the same, but how it has changed!

Revolutionary change *can* occur in America because revolutionary change *has* occurred in America. It is not too late to salvage the principle of government *by* the people and *for* the people. It is not too late for a second American revolution. But revolutionary change has always required the noisy rhetoric of preachers. So let the sons and daughters of Thomas Case stand up and shout, "Every plant which my heavenly father hath not planted must be rooted up!"

Those Who Care and Those Who Don't

Lewis Mumford has written that, "If but one person in ten were fully awakened today, fully capable of exercising his higher centers of intelligence and morality, the fatal processes that we have set in motion could be arrested, and a new direction set. . . . On that possibility mankind's security and salvation now seem to hang." [5] No one of us alone is in a position to say exactly what must be done in every situation to create a just and peaceful society. What is required is this awakening of the moral sense which Mumford speaks about in order that all of us—businessmen, lawyers, teachers, steelworkers, truckers, politicians, etc.—will come to ask, as a matter of course, not merely what we *can* do, but what we *should* do. In Christian terms, faith and obedience must be seen again as inseparable.

The psychologist Erich Fromm has said something that is very important in this regard. "What matters today," he writes, "is not the difference between those who believe and those who do not believe, but the difference between those who care and those who don't." [6]

For two thousand years, there have been those who look to Jesus and conclude that the crucial difference in the world is between those who believe and those who do not believe. It does not seem to me that this should be so; it draws the line in the wrong place. Has Jesus been so important in human history because of the things he believed and taught? Much—if not most—of what he taught was consistent with what had been taught before.

Jesus has been so important in human history because he not only believed and taught, but also *cared,* and cared profoundly. If he had not stopped to talk to blind Bartimaeus beside the road, if he had not told Zacchaeus to come down from the tree, if he had not asked the Samaritan woman for a cup of water, if he had not taken the children in his arms, if he had not allowed the harlot to touch him, if he had not placed tender hands upon the scaly bodies of lepers, if he had not spoken kindly to the thief on the cross—I would still admire his teachings, but would I be *devoted* to him? It is the contagious quality of his caring that makes the difference.

It should be very clear to us at all times that the summons to care is not a call *away* from the joys of life. To care is to know precisely those heights and depths of human existence which may not be known in any other way. The day my decision to enter the ministry was made known, that very day an acquaintance said to me, "So you've decided to be a minister. What a pity!" I must admit that in all the years since that decision was made, there have been moments when I thought he was right. But most of the time, that choice has enabled me to be with people in their joys and sorrows—and in *my* joys and sorrows—in a way which has been deeply meaningful.

A couple of years ago I was laid low by a siege of the flu which, at its peak, was utterly debilitating. I went to the upstairs bedroom and virtually defied anybody to come near me. Before too long, though, I heard the press of tiny feet on the stairs, moving upward at a very slow and cautious pace. I heard the little feet reach the top and pause for a long moment outside the closed door—which finally began to open. Before I could growl, I rolled over and found myself face to face with a two-year-old daughter who obviously had something she wanted very badly to say. She asked in the tiniest voice, "May I hurt with you, Dad?" And in her eyes I saw the hidden secrets of the universe shining like diamonds. Nothing else was said, or needed to be. She crawled into bed beside me and put her arms around me. And she taught me as no theologian had ever been able to, that caring and being cared for are the essence of what it means to be human. That caring is in no sense a burden, but rather the profoundest of joys.

When we speak of caring in this way we should not merely conjure up romantic images of ourselves following in the footsteps of an Albert Schweitzer. Rather, we should think of ourselves as businessmen and businesswomen motivated by humane values, as lawyers and judges with a passion for a just judicial system, as scientists who care more for the preservation than the exploitation of the earth, as teachers concerned with the morality of knowledge, as politicians whose integrity is not for sale at any price.

Our nation suffers, not so much from the crimes of the few, as from the indifference of the many. And all this can change when we begin to care what is happening to people. We have to care about what is happening from slum to suburb; we have to care about what is happening in jails and prisons, in convalescent homes and mental hospitals, in schools and everywhere else. Not least of all, we must continue to care about Southeast Asia and all the Third World countries in particular.

Two years ago when I was to attend a meeting in New York city, I went up a day early in the hope of spending some time in art galleries and in seeing a play. I arrived on a Sunday in the early fall, and found the city in an unusually good mood. The leaves in the parks were beautiful; there was a hint of rain carried about by a gentle breeze. It was the kind of day I needed, and I walked the streets a great deal, stopping in here and there and enjoying in anticipation the meal I was sure to have in some delicatessen with steamy windows. Then I would go to a theater to see the Broadway version of *Godspell.*

As darkness came, I stopped in front of a large old church and noticed by the sign in front that a service was in progress. I went in and saw that the cavernous structure was almost empty—maybe thirty people scattered about, none of them young. The minister was concluding a sermon in which he was impressing upon the people the notion that Satan lurked nearby at every moment of their lives, hoping to lure them away into one sort of vice or another. When he had finished, we stood and sang the old gospel hymn, "Yield not to temptation, for yielding is sin." It was a relief to get back to the street. But I noticed on the sidewalk a feeble old man, bracing himself against the wind and the rain, which by now had become hard enough to give him a struggle with his umbrella. I remembered that I had seen him before, and now he looked this way and that in obvious befuddlement. I asked him if I could help, and he told me that he could not find his way back to the hotel where he lived—and couldn't even remember the name of the place.

To make a long story short, we walked up and down those streets for at least an hour, getting soaked and hoping for some familiar landmark. During all this time, the old man spoke three lines over and over. He cursed the rain and said, "I can't understand why I am so confused." Then he said with genuine puzzlement tinged with suspicion, "Why are you being nice to me? Why would anybody do this?" At length, he remembered the name of the place, and I went about asking people where it was until I found someone who knew. We started out in that direction and as soon as he saw a familiar landmark, he broke from me, and insofar as he was able, *ran*. And I knew that there was nothing in his experience to make him risk the vulnerability of letting a stranger know exactly where he lived.

The scene will always stay with me: a large old church, persisting in patterns from which the life departed years ago, while just outside its doors a weak, lonely, lost old man fumbled about in the rain, the symbolic presence of an ocean of human agony and need in a world so unused to simple human concern that it does not recognize it when it appears.

It seems to me now that I did not find that old man on the streets of New York; I have the eerie feeling that it was he who found me. Has it ever occurred to you that for a long time now, during all the days you have rushed through your own busy streets, someone has been wandering about, looking for the way home—and calling *your* name? From the remote villages of Ecuador to the streets of Bombay starving children cry. The last sobs of somebody's grandmother faintly echo from a ditch at My Lai. A young man sticks a needle in his arm in New York. An ancient bus breaks the still silence of dawn, already filled with brown farmworkers wondering how another morning could have come so soon. From San Quentin to South Vietnam tin cups bang on bars of bamboo and steel in the desperate hope of someday creating a cacophony thunderous enough to disturb the harmony of heaven itself.

And the Presence walks among us pleading still, "Whoever has ears to hear, let them hear."

Notes

Chapter I

1. James Baldwin, *Nobody Knows My Name* (New York: Dell Publishing Company, 1961), p. 22.
2. Vine Deloria, Jr., *Custer Died for Your Sins* (New York: Macmillan, 1969), p. 106.
3. Vine Deloria, Jr., *God Is Red* (New York: Grossett & Dunlap, 1974), p. 64.
4. *Ibid.*
5. Roy I. Sano, "Toward a Liberating Ethnicity," (Oakland, California: Asian Center for Theology and Strategy, 1973), p. 1.
6. From an unsigned editorial in the *Christian Century*, 8 September 1971, p. 1039.

Chapter II

1. See Franklin H. Littell, *From State Church to Pluralism: A Protestant Interpretation of Religion in American History* (Chicago: Aldine, 1962); and Martin E. Marty, *Righteous Empire: The Protestant Experience in America* (New York: Dial Press, 1970).
2. See Will Herberg, *Protestant, Catholic, Jew: An Essay in American Religious Society* (Garden City, N. Y.: Doubleday, 1955).
3. See Robert N. Bellah's essay, "Civil Religion in America," in *Daedalus,* vol. 96 (Winter, 1967), pp. 1-21.
4. From the *San Francisco Chronicle,* 28 November 1970, p. 6.
5. William Lloyd Warner, *The Living and the Dead: A Study of the Symbolic Life of Americans* (New Haven: Yale Press, 1959), p. 279.
6. From the *New York Times,* 5 July 1970, p. 32.
7. From the *San Francisco Chronicle,* 5 February 1971, p. 5.
8. Littell, *From State Church to Pluralism,* p. xv.

Chapter III

1. Langdon Gilkey, *Naming the Whirlwind: The Renewal of God Language* (New York: Bobbs-Merrill, 1969), p. 70.
2. Michael Novak, "Social Concreteness in American Theology," in *Projections: Shaping an American Theology,* ed. Thomas F. O'Meara and Donald M. Weisser (Garden City, N. Y.: Doubleday, 1970), p. 82.
3. Marty, *Righteous Empire,* p. 31.
4. See James H. Cone, *Black Theology and Black Power* (New York: Seabury Press, 1969; *idem, A Black Theology of Liberation* (New York: J. B. Lippincott, 1970); and *idem,* "Christian Theology and the Afro-American Revolution," *Christianity and Crisis* 30, no. 10 (8 June 1970), 123-25.
5. Cone, *Black Theology and Black Power,* p. 115.

Chapter IV

1. See H. Richard Niebuhr, *Christ and Culture* (New York: Harper & Row, 1951).
2. Cone, *A Black Theology of Liberation,* pp. 49, 51-2.
3. See Harold Cruse, *The Crisis of the Negro Intellectual,* (New York: Morrow, 1967); *idem, Rebellion or Revolution* (New York: Morrow, 1968).
4. David L. Lewis, *King: A Critical Biography* (New York: Praeger, 1970), p. 354.
5. Theodore Roszak, *The Making of a Counter Culture* (Garden City, N.Y.: Doubleday-Anchor, 1969), pp. 55, 4-5.
6. Charles A. Reich, *The Greening of America* (New York: Random House, 1970), p. 57.
7. Philip Slater, *The Pursuit of Loneliness: American Culture at the Breaking Point* (Boston: Beacon Press, 1970).

Chapter V

1. Charles H. Anderson, *White Protestant Americans: From National Origins to Religious Group* (Englewood Cliffs, N. J.: Prentice-Hall, 1970), p .1.
2. Vine Deloria, Jr., *We Talk, You Listen: New Tribes, New Turf* (New York: Macmillan, 1970), pp. 138-52.
3. Deloria, *Custer Died for Your Sins,* p. 37.
4. Deloria, *We Talk, You Listen,* p. 106.
5. Robert W. Terry, *For Whites Only* (Grand Rapids, Michigan: Eerdman's, 1970), pp. 20, 34.

Chapter VI

1. From the *San Francisco Chronicle*, 2 February 1971, p. 8.
2. See Tom Wolfe, *Radical Chic and Mau-Mauing the Flak Catchers* (New York: Bantam, 1970).
3. John B. Orr and F. Patrick Nichelson, *The Radical Suburb: Soundings in Changing American Character* (Philadelphia: Westminster, 1970), p. 182.

Chapter VII

1. Arthur Miller, *Death of a Salesman* (New York: Viking Press, 1949), p. 48.
2. *Ibid.*, p. 138.
3. Martin Luther, *The Large Catechism of Martin Luther*, trans. Robert H. Fischer (Philadelphia: Muhlenberg Press, 1959), p. 9.
4. From my own seminary lecture notes.
5. Viktor Frankl, *Man's Search for Meaning* (New York: Washington Square Press, 1963), p. 172.
6. Dag Hammarskjöld, *Markings* (New York: Alfred A. Knopf, 1964), p. xii.
7. Rudolf Bultmann, *Jesus Christ and Mythology* (New York: Scribner's, 1958), p. 40.
8. Archibald MacLeish, *J.B.* (Cambridge, Mass., Riverside Press, 1956), p. 14.
9. Daniel Day Williams, *The Spirit and the Forms of Love* (New York: Harper & Row, 1968), p. 185.
10. Allen Ginsberg, *Howl, and Other Poems* (San Francisco: City Lights Books, 1956), pp. 26-7.
11. Quoted in *Jonathan Edwards: A Profile*, ed. David Levin (New York: Hill and Wang, 1969), p. 27.
12. Miguel de Unamuno, *The Tragic Sense of Life*, trans. J. E. Crawford Flitch (New York: Dover, 1954), p. 184.

Chapter VIII

1. See John Nordheimer, "The Tragedy of a Gentle Hero," in the *San Francisco Chronicle*, 29 May 1971, p. 6.
2. *New York Times*, 28 March 1960, p. 55.
3. Quoted by Martin E. Marty in *Context*, 1 February 1974 (Chicago: Thomas More Association), p. 1.
4. Lewis Mumford, *The Conduct of Life* (New York: Harcourt, Brace & Company, 1957), pp. 170-71.

5. See Samuel S. Hill, *Southern Churches in Crisis* (Boston: Beacon, 1968).

6. Willie Morris, *North Toward Home* (New York: Harper's Magazine Press, 1967), p. 50.

7. Wade Crawford Barclay, *History of Methodist Missions,* Early American Methodism, vol. 2 (New York: Board of Missions and Church Extension of The Methodist Church, 1950), p. 3.

8. Tony Fitch and Julian Tepper, "The Politics of Prisons," *Christianity and Crisis* 31, no. 17 (18 October 1971), 219.

9. See "Justice on Trial," *Newsweek,* 8 March 1971, p. 17.

10. Donald G. Shockley, "Imprisoning the Poor," *Christian Century,* 28 October 1970, p. 1286.

11. Albert Camus, *The Fall* (New York: Alfred A. Knopf, 1957) p. 84.

12. Gary Wills, quoted by Martin E. Marty in *Context,* December 1, 1973 (Chicago: Thomas More Association), p. 5.

13. Karl Menninger, *Whatever Became of Sin* (New York: Hawthorn, 1973), p. 188.

14. Reinhold Niebuhr quoted in Menninger, pp. 135-136.

Chapter IX

1. Avery Dulles, "Incarnation 1973: Reflections at Christmas," *Commonweal,* 28 December 1973, p. 335.

Chapter X

1. Michael Walazer, *The Revolution of the Saints* (Cambridge, Mass.: Harvard University Press, 1965), p. 125.

2. Slater, *The Pursuit of Loneliness,* pp. 126-28.

3. William Stringfellow, "Jesus the Criminal," *Christianity and Crisis* 30, no. 10 (1970), 119-22.

4. Walzer, *Revolution of the Saints,* pp. 10-11.

5. Mumford, *The Conduct of Life,* pp. 118-19.

6. Erich Fromm, *The Revolution of Hope* (New York: Harper & Row, 1968), p. 135.